VET TAILS

VET TAILS

SMALL STORIES FROM A SMALL TOWN,
SMALL ANIMAL VETERINARIAN

BY CHARLIE FREED, DVM

TATE PUBLISHING & *Enterprises*

Published by Tate Publishing & Enterprises, LLC
127 E. Trade Center Terrace | Mustang, Oklahoma 73064 USA
1.888.361.9473 | www.tatepublishing.com

Tate Publishing is committed to excellence in the publishing industry. The company reflects the philosophy established by the founders, based on Psalm 68:11,
"The Lord gave the word and great was the company of those who published it."

Book design copyright © 2008 by Tate Publishing, LLC. All rights reserved.
Cover design by Jacob Crissup
Interior design by Summer Floyd Harvey

Published in the United States of America

ISBN: 978-1-60604-504-6
1. Biography & Autobiography: Medical: Physicians
2. Medical: Veterinary Medicine: Small Animal
08.09.18

DEDICATION

My Mom and Dad, Dorothy and Peter, who gave me patience.

My classmate, Ivan George Pollack, DVM, who gave me friendship.

My wife, Frances, who gives me love.

My employees, clients, and patients who gave me these stories.

ACKNOWLEDGEMENT

In December 2005, Eric and April Hoggatt, owners and publishers of the *Willits' Nickel & Dime,* asked me if I would be willing to write a weekly article about Veterinary Medicine. We discussed what the possibilities were, considering a question and answer format. At that time I'd had a few of my short stories published in veterinary trade journals and asked if they would consider that; they agreed. I told them I could probably write one story a month for about six months. So began my fifteen minutes of fame writing short stories for the *Willits' Nickel & Dime.* By March of 2007, I had sixteen short stories in print and one had been selected as the short story of 2007 in Veterinary Economics. I began wondering if anyone else might be interested in my stories. *Vet Tails* came out of that experience, and I'd like to thank Eric and April Hoggatt for giving me the impetus to start this book of stories.

I would also like to thank the following people for their ideas, suggestions, and help with this book; their advice and comments were most appreciated:

Rebecca Sandridge
Del Nagel
Maggie Graham
Gene Stewart
Bruce Haanstra
John Hoggatt
Michele Collicott
Ron Moorhead
Bob Anderson, DVM
Lynn Kennelly
Art Eck
Amy Wray
Triple-S Camera Shop
Tracy Livingston
The Willits News (for the pictures of Creamery)
The Willits Library

Table of Contents

Introduction

I have always felt that the best doctor in the world
is the Veterinarian.

Will Rogers

Hi, my name is Charlie A. Freed; I'd like to take you on
a short journey. I'm a veterinarian practicing in Willits,
California. I've been practicing for thirty-four years
and I'm still working full-time. I graduated from Ventura High School in 1967, from Ventura Junior College
in 1969, from U. C. Davis undergraduate school in 1970,
and from the School of Veterinary Medicine at U. C.
Davis in 1974.

Veterinary Medicine has been a great career; I've
seen things, met people, worked on all kinds of pets;
what a life it's been. The strange thing about life is that
if I'd known it would turn out so well, I wouldn't have
spent so much time worrying about it when I was young.
What would I do with my life? Where would I live? Would

I find someone to share life with? All the things young people worry about.

By seventh grade, I'd already decided I was going to be a veterinarian. In junior college it was difficult to find the requirements for the veterinary medicine program so I made an appointment with a counselor at U. C. Davis to help plan my classes. I believe that one trip ensured my entrance into veterinary school.

After graduation from U. C. Davis I practiced in the Bay Area for four years and finally bought a veterinary clinic in Willits, California, in 1978 where I've been ever since.

In the following pages, I'd like to share with you some of the people and their pets that have made my career so fascinating and ever changing. There is more to tell, but I hope this will give you a glimpse at how special and rewarding my job is. I can tell you right off, it's not a nine to five job and it's never boring. Come along and I hope you'll let me know if you enjoy these stories.

CHARLIE A. FREED, DVM

ONE DAY

1976

Tuesday, 4:00 p.m.: Davenport cat, Honey, routine vaccinations.

I held the Davenport's cat, Honey, firmly, trying to keep her from climbing up my face. Her front claws gripped my tie; so the more I pulled her away from me the tighter my tie became. I was losing oxygen.

"Dr. Freed! You're scaring poor Honey!" Mr. and Mrs. Davenport stood across the exam room but made no attempt to help me. All I could think was I didn't want Honey's claws reaching my face. While holding her tightly with my right hand I tried to dislodge her nails from my tie with my left hand.

"Poor Honey. Dr. Freed, you're hurting her! Please, can't you be gentler? Poor, poor Honey. It's okay, Honey we won't let that mean doctor hurt you."

I mentally closed my eyes. *Ah, another wonderful day.*

Earlier That Morning

Tuesday, 7:30 a.m.

Working at the Irvine Veterinary Hospital in San Bruno, California, these last two years had been an eye opener. Nothing I'd studied or seen in veterinary school could've prepared me for the clients who entered through the front door.

My morning began at 5:30 a.m. I awoke in my apartment, showered, shaved, and dressed, had some toast and coffee and began the drive to the Irvine Veterinary Clinic, a one-hour drive if the traffic wasn't bad. I pulled out of the apartment complex driving slowly through the neighborhood making my way to 280, the freeway that would take me into San Bruno.

As I turned down Thirty-Second Avenue I noticed a beautiful Golden Retriever making his rounds of the fine trimmed lawns and hedges of the houses that lined this quiet residential street. He gracefully turned and crossed the street just ahead of me when all of a sudden he started to shake, stumble, and fall onto his right side, jerking uncontrollably. I stopped my car and ran up to him. As he flailed back and forth, frothing at the mouth, I cradled his head so he won't injure himself

"You hit Sir Raleigh!" I heard from the sidewalk. "Stop! Bruce! Call the Jefferys! This man just hit Sir Raleigh!"

I looked up to see a woman in a lime-green fuzzy housecoat, coffee cup in one hand, yelling to an open door behind her. "Ma'am, I didn't hit him. He's having a seizure."

"You wait right there young man, I'm going for some paper and pen to write your name down. I'll get your car license number too!"

She bustled into the house.

"But...I didn't hit him!"

Neighbors were now coming out of their houses on both sides of the street and stared at me malevolently. I felt Sir Raleigh beginning to relax, and as he looked up at me, I could see he was starting to recognize his surroundings again. He tried to get up but fell.

"What's your name?" She was back—paper and pen in hand, with her husband in his pajamas, coffee cup steaming, glaring over her shoulder.

"Look, I'm a veterinarian. This dog just had a seizure, and I can tell he is coming around."

"You wait right there." She walked toward my car for my license number.

I looked down at Sir Raleigh pleading with him to get up and prove me right. He licked my face.

In unison the neighbors were closing in; were the Jefferys soon to arrive? I shivered at the thought. I walked quickly back to my car and got in as the house-coat lady wrote vigorously.

I could see that Sir Raleigh was getting up and saw the crowd standing around him to access the damage.

As I drove past I called from my open window, "He had a grand mal seizure! I didn't hit him!"

They raised their fists and shouted at me. I couldn't wait to get to work.

EARLY BEGINNINGS

Possess your soul with patience.

-THE HIND AND THE PANTHER

1966

Life hadn't always been like this. I could remember my school days in Ventura where I was the neighborhood expert with animals of all sorts. It wasn't that I had any special knowledge, but I'd had a lot of unusual pets over the years: a California dove, an owl, a squirrel, one tarantula, and two bats—among others. One of my hobbies was collecting dead animals I found and putting their skeletons together in our family's garage.

I'd been working on a dead squirrel I'd found two days before. It was under my dad's workbench; it wasn't a pleasant odor.

"What is that awful smell, Charlie?" My mother asked.

"It's that squirrel I found on Canyon Pass Road."

"It smells awful, your dad isn't going to be happy about this. Why don't you bury that poor thing?"

"But, Mom, I just need to soak it in some chlorine bleach solution then I can start cleaning it up."

She was holding her apron over her mouth, but I could see her eyes. "Well, keep the door open to air the garage out before your dad gets home."

"Okay, Mom. Once it's soaking you'll hardly notice it." She was staring at me and her eyes gleamed with desperation.

I picked up the dead squirrel and removed some of the tissue that was just hanging.

"Oh my..." She hurried toward the house.

I smiled. Now I was alone to begin my project. I lowered it into the bleach solution, covered it, and in two days would begin the careful dissecting.

At the moment I had a hawk skeleton on my bureau, a cat skull that I'd made into a night light by my bed, but my most recent project was assembling a complete cow skeleton in my bedroom. I'd anchored its spine to hang from the ceiling and one by one cleaned and wired each bone, following a book I'd borrowed from the Ventura Library.

My mother tolerated my hobby as long as I kept it confined to my room; she even dusted the cow skeleton when she cleaned. Both of my parents were very patient with all my various pets and projects.

Wednesday nights my mother entertained a group of her friends for their weekly game of Pinochle. There was Mrs. Turner, Mrs. Cameron, Mrs. Twindlin, Mrs. Valdine, Ms. Littleton, and my mom. Ms. Littleton was a retired elementary school teacher, Mrs. Valdine was a bookkeeper, Mrs. Twindlin was the wife of our Methodist minister, and Mrs. Cameron was the vice-principal of the elementary school (where Ms. Littleton had worked for twenty-seven years), and Mrs. Turner was our next door neighbor.

Ms. Littleton, a refined woman, hadn't married. She dressed elegantly, even wearing white gloves, her hair always in a permanent, and she wore narrow glasses with silver rims, which gave her an intimidating look.

"Charlie, the ladies will be here shortly. Where are Desi and Lucy?" My mom called from the hallway.

I'd obtained Desi and Lucy a month ago. Mrs. Thomas, the librarian at the local elementary school that I'd just graduated from, had been concerned about two bats that got into her library. They'd fly around from time to time, but she didn't know what to do about it. Ralph Emerson, the custodian, had failed trying to net them. I knew quite a lot about bats having completed a school project only the year before.

Approaching her one day, I said, "I could catch them for you, Mrs. Thomas."

She smiled and looked down at me. "You, Charlie?"

"Sure."

"Charlie, Mr. Emerson has tried many times and hasn't been able to catch them."

"I can do it."

Mrs. Thomas sat down next to me. "And just how would you do that, Charlie?"

"Would you let me do it?"

"I'd have to get the approval from Mr. Williamson."

(That would be the principal. I didn't think that would be a good idea.) "And your mother."

Now I was smiling. "You can call my mom, Mrs. Thomas. She'll tell you I can do it, but do you really need to bother Mr. Williamson?"

"I'll call your mom first."

I knew she thought my mom would say no, but I couldn't help Mrs. Thomas thinking that. She didn't know my mom.

That night, after dinner, I went down to the school. Everyone was gone. I took my flash light out and shined it at the window into the library. I could see the bats flying by, swooping at the light.

After awhile I turned the flash light off, staring into the dimly lit library. I watched the bats circle and swoop then swiftly they flew up to the far bookcase, against the wall, and disappeared over the top.

Two days later I was back at the library. "I'll catch those bats tomorrow morning for you, Mrs. Thomas. I'll be here at eight a.m. sharp!"

"Well, Charlie, your mom said you could do it, and I'm afraid one of the students will get bitten, so we have to do something. You're sure you can catch them?"

I nodded my head. Not only was I sure, I already had a place for them set up in my bedroom. The next morning I was waiting by the library door with my jar when Mrs. Thomas walked up.

"Good morning, Charlie. What's in the jar?"

"Nothing, but there soon will be."

We went into the library and turned all the lights on. I rolled the book ladder and positioned it so I could get to the top shelf. I placed my jar on the top and started to pull myself up.

"Mrs. Thomas! What's going on here?" Mr. Williamson had just walked in. "Charlie, get down from there this instant."

I froze. Mrs. Thomas didn't look well.

"I think I see that book, Mrs. Thomas. It's wedged down behind the bookcase. I can get it."

"Charlie, get the book and then get down from there. Mrs. Thomas don't leave Charlie until he is safely on the floor. And next time call Ralph to do that."

We were both relieved when he walked out.

"Hurry, Charlie. Can you see them?"

I was looking down at two sleeping brown, leathery California myotis bats. "Oh, yes, I can see them, Mrs. Thomas."

I reached down with my gloved hand and picked them up one at a time. They opened their mouths and bit my glove, but their teeth were tiny. Their faces looked like miniature foxes.

"How did you do that Charlie? How'd you know where they'd be?"

"There're bats. They like small crevices to hide, that was the only likely place." There was no need to tell her about my visit the other night.

My mom was waiting in the parking lot. A fast trip home to put Desi and Lucy into their new home and then off to school for me.

Desi and Lucy soon found themselves flying around my room at night while I did my homework. I would toss insects and moths into the air for them to catch. They liked to hang from the stucco ceiling where they would wrap the insect into their tail web and then, hanging upside down, they would put their heads into the tail web to eat.

So now, my mom's weekly card game was about to start and Desi and Lucy were moving about in their cage wondering why they hadn't been let out yet. I was talking to them while I prepared the jar of insects when my eyes glanced by my red tarantula, Violet's, terrarium. The lid was skewed. I looked into the terrarium checking her hiding space. She was gone! I futilely searched my room, but Violet wasn't to be found. Worriedly, I walked down the hall into the living room.

To my horror Violet had positioned herself on the edge of the couch only three feet from Mrs. Littleton.

"Good evening, everybody."

My mom already knew something was up, and I watched her scan the room, checking the ceiling first.

"Hello, Charlie. My you're getting tall," Mrs. Valdine said.

My mom's eyes enlarged when she saw Violet. I walked over and sat down between Mrs. Littleton and Violet, closer to Violet.

"And how is school going this year, Charles." Ms. Littleton always called me Charles.

"Really well. I like algebra, and I'm reading Moby Dick in English." I edged my arm up to Violet who placed one leg on it as I began to move over; I'd turned my body slightly to block the view. Violet had to feel each area as she slowly worked her way up my arm and into the pocket of my shirt. I saw my mom breathe a sigh of relief as Violet was hidden from view.

"Well, I'd better get back to my homework."

"Good night, Charles."

The women adjourned to the dinning room where my mom had the table set up. Violet was placed back into her home and my door was shut. All was calm, no problems tonight. Finally, I let Desi and Lucy out and got back to my studies.

Moments later my dad opened the door. "Good night, Charlie." Desi and Lucy saw their opportunity. "Oh my..."

We both looked hopelessly as they flew down the hallway into the living room. I watched my dad make a fast retreat to his bedroom.

Screams, cups crashing, and then the inevitable cry from my mom, "*Charlie!*"

THE INTERVIEW

And lean upon the thought that chance will bring
us through.

-Empedocles on Etna

1969

I had one more year at Ventura Junior College so I
decided to go up to U. C. Davis to find out what classes
I still needed for entrance into Veterinary School.

I called the Student Affairs Department, and they assigned a professor to give me some guidance. His name was Dr. Paul Griddle, and I had an appointment to meet him at 1:30 p.m. on August 22.

It was 103 degrees as I pulled my 1965 Volkswagen with no air-conditioning into a large parking lot just in front of the gates to the campus. I was sweaty, wet, and tired, and I was still in my car. I opened the door and stood trying to get my bearings. The campus was larger than I'd thought, and I'd no idea where Haring Hall was. I straightened my tie and put on my sport jacket and with map in hand I began walking.

As I walked, I realized I'd parked further away from Haring Hall then I needed to. My feet felt like they were in water as I squished my way down the sidewalks under the afternoon sun. My shirt was sticking to my back, and my tie was beginning to feel like a noose. I wouldn't look very cool and collected for this interview.

I found Haring Hall, and it was awe-inspiring to someone from a little community college. It was a two-story, white-stone building with a large stone mural on the front wall. I walked into the foyer. Looking up at the high ceiling, the walls were covered with pictures of past administrators beginning in 1950. I felt a feeling of tradition, a tradition I wanted to be part of. Once inside, I went to the nearest bathroom and looked in the mirror. My face was bright red, and my hair was wet and hung down. I washed my face and dried my hair holding my head under the hand dryer. I looked totally wasted. Why had I worn this jacket? I combed my hair and decided I had to give this interview my best, but I wasn't sure I was up to it.

I practiced what I'd say as I walked down the long hallway looking for room 104. *Good afternoon Dr. Griddle. I really appreciate your seeing me today.* I would then give him a firm handshake and stand up straight.

I stood outside the door. The window was opaque and in big letters "Pathology Department" was stenciled in the middle.

I opened the door and walked in. A man of about fifty was leaning over a microscope. He wore thick glasses; his black hair was mostly gray and beginning to thin on top. His clean, pressed, long-sleeved, white lab coat went past his knees.

"Yes?" he asked without looking up.

"Hello." I moved into the room and closed the door. "My name is Charlie Freed, and I have an appointment with Dr. Griddle at one thirty p.m."

"Oh, yes. I'm Dr. Griddle." He stood up and

walked forward. I extended my right hand to introduce myself.

"Good afternoon Dr. Griddle. I really..." It was while my hand was thrust out in front of me that I noticed Dr. Griddle's right hand wasn't there. In its place was a shiny, stainless steel prosthesis with a double action hook. He looked at me, and I slowly put my hand down. I was wishing I could start over.

He then smiled. "That's all right." He motioned me towards his desk. "Here, Mr. Freed, please take a seat. You're from Ventura?"

I sat down opposite him. "That's right. Please call me, Charlie."

As he listened to me, he produced a pipe that he expertly handled and lit, holding the pipe with his prosthesis. After his pipe was going well, he continued. "I believe you're graduating from Junior College next year?"

"Yes, sir. I'll finish up with my AA degree, but I still have some classes for my prerequisites that weren't offered at Ventura. What should I do?"

"Did you bring your transcripts with you?"

I pulled out my papers and handed them to Dr. Griddle. He took some time going through them and making notes. He then pulled a binder out and went through it. It looked like he was comparing classes. Finally he looked up.

"Well Charlie, you've done quite well, and I only see three classes that are needed. One is Genetics, and the others are Comparative Anatomy and Animal Husbandry. I think you should go ahead and apply to the veterinary school. Send them these transcripts." He handed me the notes he had taken. "Use these notes to explain that you intend to spend a year at U. C. fulfilling the final requirements. I will send the Dean of Students a letter on your behalf."

"You would do that for me?"

He smiled and drew on his pipe; smoke spiraled up to the ceiling.

"Did you drive up from Ventura today?"

"Yes. I left at four o' clock this morning."

"And you're driving back today?"

"Yes. I only have today off. I'm working this summer."

"You must really want to be a vet?"

"Oh yes, Dr. Griddle."

Some more smoke rose upward. "Then that's what you'll be."

Genetics

But times do change and move continually.
                                        -THE FAERIE QUEENE

1970

My first day of classes at U. C. Davis was nothing like what I'd experienced at Ventura College. I walked pass the five-story library, the dorms, the chemistry building, the original animal husbandry building next to Haring Hall where many of my classes would be taught, and still, the campus spread out in all directions. The campus had its own police department, fire department, and health center. When school was in session, there were over twenty thousand students. The campus was a city within a city, and I felt swallowed up by it.

The classes at Ventura College of twenty to thirty students were no comparison to my classes here of one hundred to two hundred students. One such class was Genetics, and I remember the first day very well.

Genetics 103 was a five-unit class. This was one of the classes not offered at Ventura College, and it would be the largest unit class I'd be taking that year. I had to pass this class to complete the units needed to get into the veterinary school the following year. The book was huge, and the wording incomprehensible; it was going to be a difficult class.

I remember walking up the stairs to the large glass doors and entering the lobby. There were four doors, which opened into a vast room. I saw the equivalent of two stories going down from where I stood. The front of the classroom was so far away that it looked miniature. The walls had television sets mounted so the students could see the professor and what was written on the black board. I decided to sit in the front row.

Students began filling the lecture hall, and it seemed that there were more students in this one class then the whole student body from my junior college. These students looked older or maybe more experienced to college life. I felt like a minnow in this pond, feeling insecure and worried. A scruffy looking man sat down next to me.

"Looks like it'll be a full classroom," he said to me as he looked back to the expanse of the room.

I briefly looked at him with his uncombed hair and wrinkled clothes, "Yeah." I was wearing slacks and a dress shirt.

He looked through his book, "Are you looking forward to Genetics this semester?"

Why was this guy talking to me? "No. I have to take this class to get into Veterinary School. It's a requirement."

"Oh?" He opened his book to a page and was holding his finger on it to keep his place. "I think Genetics is fascinating. It applies to so many things in our daily lives."

What planet was this guy from? I was looking to change my seat, but the room had filled and there were no empty seats. "It looks like a bunch of useless stuff. I don't think this will be a very fun class." I smugly told him.

"Well the classroom is full I guess it's probably time to start." He was straightening his books on his desk.

I looked over at him. "Well, there's no professor here so I guess it'll be a while. I could've had another cup of coffee if I knew the professor was going to be late."

He looked over at me. "Just a class to get into Veterinary School? Do you want to be a veterinarian?"

It was time to let this guy know whom he was talking to. "Well, I was going to join the Army with my high school buddies, but right before they joined up I got an acceptance letter from the Veterinary School. All I need to do is take a few classes that weren't available at the junior college. I'm looking forward to Animal Husbandry and Comparative Anatomy, but Genetics..."

He stood up. *Good, he's finally leaving me alone. Good riddance,* I thought.

He turned to face me, "I better get going." He turned from me and walked to the front of the class. He proceeded to write on the black board, Genetics 103, and then his name, Henry Lavoire. He turned to face us. "Good morning and welcome to Genetics 103. If you are in the wrong room now is the time to leave. For those of you in the correct room it's time to start. Now, I know some of you," and he looked directly at me, "are only here because you are forced to take Genetics 103 as a requirement. But for the others I know you'll enjoy this class as much as I enjoy teaching it. Let's begin."

I was feeling woozy. I was getting a stomachache.

The Pig Project

A little work, a little play, to keep us going and so, good day!

TRILBY

In the summer of 1971, between classes at the Veterinary School, I got a job working for the university. It was a study to conduct the effects of overcrowding on weight gain for meat production in pigs. They called it the Pig Project. There were two enclosures each with thirty-five pigs. It was my job to clean and feed them, but (and here was the catch) I couldn't move them out of the enclosure when I cleaned them. They had to be in this particular enclosure for the length of the study. It wasn't too bad to go into their enclosure as long as you didn't try to bring in food. One day I'd just finished cleaning the enclosures and was walking over to the feed storage to make up the various feeds for the pigs, when I saw Mr. Daniels, my supervisor, and Popeye talking. Popeye was holding a little piglet.

Popeye was in his sixties and had been working as a ranch hand for U. C. Davis since his twenties. He stood six foot three and weighed a good 280. His hands were half the size of my head. Popeye was a great source of information, which he readily dispensed. I stood to the side as they talked.

"So this one has it too?" Mr. Daniels was looking at the piglet Popeye held and was palpating its joints.

Popeye shifted the squirming piglet. "Yep, makes five so far. I think the floor is too rough, and they are picking up an infection." Mr. Daniels was shaking his head.

"Take care of this one, Popeye, and I'll talk with the professors and see what they want to do. At this rate the study will be over from lack of numbers." Popeye was shaking his head and his eyes caught mine. Mr. Daniels looked at me as he walked past.

"Don't you have any work to do, Charlie?"

"Yes, sir. I'm just getting ready to make up the feeds for lots twenty-three and twenty-four."

"Well, don't let me stop you."

"What?" Popeye shook his head at me. "I mean, yes, sir. I'll get right to it."

I went into the next barn and picked up two buckets and put them in the wheelbarrow. I was scooping up some feed when Popeye walked in still holding the piglet. "You doing okay, Charlie? Do you need some help?"

"Yeah, I'm doing okay. What's up with the little pig?"

Popeye held the piglet so its front legs extended towards me. Its tiny wrists were very swollen. "She has a joint infection. She can't walk enough to eat so she is out of the study group."

I walked over to look at the pig and then looked up at Popeye. "What happens to her now?" Popeye turned away from me and started to walk out of the barn. I ran up behind him. "Popeye?" He stopped walking but didn't turn around. I walked around in front of him. "Popeye?"

"I have to put her down."

"But why? Just because her joints are swollen?"

"Well Charlie, she can't be in the study group now, and there's really no place for her. The cost to treat her isn't realistic for the college. She's not needed anymore." Clearly Popeye wasn't relishing the task ahead.

"I could do it."

Popeye looked down at me. "You could do what?"

"I could take care of her."

"You don't know the first thing about it. She needs

antibiotics, warm-water soaks, soft bedding, feeding. Why, there's a whole lot of work to be done and then what? Nobody wants her anyway."

"I do."

Popeye sat down on a bale of hay. "Charlie, even if you did this, where would you keep her?"

I knew I had no right to speak up, but darn that piglet was just too cute. She was black with a wide white stripe around her belly, a Hampshire.

"Well?" Popeye was stroking the little pig.

"You could tell me what to do, and then I could come out here every day and take care of her, and on the weekends I could spend the whole day with her. I could keep her down in the barn where I have my truck."

"And when the school term ends, then what?"

"I'll have a year to find her a good home."

Popeye considered this for a while. "And who is going to tell Mr. Daniels?"

"I will."

Popeye stood up. "Come on, Charlie, let me show you something."

I followed Popeye into the "kitchen" where we kept refrigerated supplies, medicines and our lunches.

Popeye handed the piglet to me. "Hold this little thing for me." He reached into the refrigerator and pulled out a bottle of penicillin-streptomycin and rooted around the cupboards until he found a syringe and needle. "See this bottle?" I nodded. "You need to give her one-half cc every day. Then you need to soak her joints in warm water, then rub this liniment on her joints and make sure she is on soft bedding. Clean soft bedding."

"I can do that, Popeye."

He had me hold the piglet while he gave her a shot. Boy did she squeal!

I took her down to the barn where my truck was parked. Three months before my truck's starter had broke, and I was still saving up money to buy a new one. I put the piglet in a stall in the very back of the barn, hoping Mr. Daniels wouldn't see her and fixed her up with some fresh straw. I then mixed up some gruel and put it down for her, and as I walked out of the barn, she was eating vigorously.

And so began my two-month mission of riding my bicycle over to the barn each morning, giving Sue, as I'd named her, her shot, feeding her and then on to work. In the evening, I'd put Sue in a big sink full of warm water and massaged her legs. Then after drying her off, I'd rub the liniment on her joints. Sue really enjoyed her warm water soaks. On the weekends she would follow me around when I was working out in the barn. When I worked on my truck, she would crawl under it and lie next to me.

One Saturday as I was working on my truck, I saw Mr. Daniels' feet approaching. I looked over at Sue; she was sleeping. "Oh, please, Sue, just keep sleeping," I whispered.

"Charlie?"

I didn't dare move because I was afraid Sue would wake up. "Yes, sir, Mr. Daniels."

"When are you going to get this truck out of here?"

"I'm working on that right now. I have the old starter out, and I need to run into Sacramento to get a new one. I'd say within the next two weeks."

"Well, alright then. I'll need the space soon to store feed for the winter." I watched his feet walk away. "And Charlie."

"Yes, Mr. Daniels?"

"You'll need to find another place to keep Sue."

I looked down at Sue. She was now lying on her back. I rubbed her stomach and she nuzzled my arm but kept on sleeping.

The days went by, and Sue's little legs were definitely getting better. I was eating my lunch one Saturday in the "kitchen" when Popeye came in.

"Hi, Popeye."

He walked over to the refrigerator and took out an old scratched-up milk bottle with a piece of foil for a lid. He pealed back the foil and began drinking. "Hey." He came over and sat down. "Want some milk? Fresh today, I milked her myself."

"No, thanks anyway," I said holding up the Pepsi I was drinking.

"Sue seems to be doing better. You doing okay with her?"

I smiled. "She's doing great and really getting big now. She follows me around like a dog."

"Pigs are good." He was quiet for a while, too quiet.

"Popeye?"

He looked up at me. "You have to move her."

"I know. Mr. Daniels already told me."

"I mean real soon."

"Why? What's up?"

"At the end of every summer all the guys out here have a barbecue. It's a big deal. Wives, family, the bosses. They all show up."

"So?"

"So the guys have been eyeing Sue. They see how well you've been feeding her, and there is talk."

"*No!*"

Popeye stood up. "You've got to move her, Charlie. And soon." He walked out the door pulling on his gloves.

The next week I was ready to move Sue to the Sheep Barn. I rode my bike over to the barn where I kept her, gave her a banana, and soon she was trotting alongside my bike as I pedaled over to the Sheep Barn at the Veterinary Medical Teaching Hospital.

Dr. Dans was my professor for my large animal rotation, and although he knew I was small animal bound, treated me no differently. Some of the large animal professors would ignore students in their rotation if they knew you were going into small animal medicine. They would give the messy and unpleasant tasks to us. But Dr. Dans was different; he didn't make judgments. I'd explained my problem to him the week before.

"Until the end of the term Charlie, then she has to go. You can use the far stall in the Sheep Barn, but it has to be kept clean. You have to do that."

"I will Dr. Dans. I'll take care of Sue and feed her and clean the stall."

He gave me a sign to put on Sue's stall. "Study Project, Sophomore Student, Do Not Move, See Dr. Dans."

He walked away. It was the beginning of my admiration of this professor.

• • • •

I finally had the money for the new starter. Jim Lavely was a classmate who was also living in the Graduate Rooms that year. He'd heard me asking for a ride into Sacramento to pick up a starter.

"You need a ride?"

"Are you going into Sacramento?"

"No."

"Oh."

"But I've a car you can use."

"Oh, Jim, that would be great. It won't take me long, just down to Sacramento and back."

"I don't need my car today, Charlie, you can use it as long as you like. It's the blue Ford out there."

He was holding some keys.

I went out to the parking lot and walked up and down the rows looking at the makes and colors of all the cars. I didn't see any blue Ford. On my fourth trip down the rows my eyes stared at a 1969 Ford Mustang Mach I. *Nah,* I said to myself. But it's blue and it's a Ford. The Mustang had a wide white stripe running down the center. I walked over to the car and put the key into the door latch. It *turned!* I couldn't believe anyone would loan out such a beautiful car. I got into the driver's seat and turned the key. *What a sound!* And what a ride to Sacramento and back. I thanked Jim for letting me to use his car, but he acted like it was no big deal.

• • • •

Behind the Sheep Barn and across the road is Putah Creek. In the evening Sue and I would walk along the creek, watching the ducks. Sometimes people would pass by in canoes. I kept treats in my jacket pockets for Sue to nibble on. I'd lie down on the grass, and Sue would lie down next to me and roll over to have her belly rubbed. She especially liked me to scratch behind her ears. Some of the students would stop and talk to Sue, others canoeing by would wave and say hi.

As the college term began to come to a close, I

intensified my attempts to find a home for Sue. Most of the people who responded to my ad made me too suspicious of their intentions so I turned them down. One day when I was in the Dean of Students' Office, the receptionist, Mrs. Prinekles, asked me about Sue.

"Charlie, have you found a home for Sue?"

"Not yet, but I still have some time. Do you know anyone who'd give her a good home?"

Mrs. Prinekles motioned me over to her desk. "Charlie, how does Sue act. Is she mean?"

"Oh no, Mrs. Prinekles. She loves having her ears scratched, and she will do anything for a banana." This made Mrs. Prinekles smile.

"You see, Charlie, I have a son, Michael. He has Down's syndrome, and he just lost his dog, Tippy. He wants a horse, but I am afraid that would be just a little more than we could handle. We do have a small barn, a corral, and a well fenced yard on some property just outside Dixon."

"I think Sue would be happy there. Did I mention she likes to be sprayed with water? Maybe you could bring Michael over to see her sometime. I have her out in the Sheep Barn."

"I know."

"You know?"

"Charlie, I think everyone knows what you've been up to. I hope you've thanked Dr. Dans for pulling all the right strings for you and Sue."

"What do you mean?"

"Dr. Dans has done a lot of explaining why there's a pig in the Sheep Barn. Dean Thomas has been pretty hard on him, but Dr. Dans has persuaded the Dean that Sue is a good learning tool for you and the other students on that rotation. Some of the conversations have gotten quite spirited, I can tell you."

"I had no idea. Dr. Dans has never said a word to me about it."

She shuffled some papers on her desk. "No, he wouldn't."

"I'll be sure to talk with Dr. Dans and let him know how much this has meant to me and Sue."

Mrs. Prinekles stood up and put her hand on my shoulder. "That would be a good idea. So, would Saturday be alright to bring Michael over to see Sue?"

"Yes, ma'am. What time?"

"Let's say ten a.m.?"

"I'll be there. Thank you, Mrs. Prinekles. Thank you very much."

"Now Charlie, I haven't committed myself yet. Let's see what Michael and Sue think."

• • • •

The week went fast, and on Saturday morning I had Sue's stall cleaned and had given her a bath by the time Mr. and Mrs. Prinekles and their son, Michael, drove up. Michael looked to be about fifteen and I was introduced.

"Where is Sue?" Michael asked right off. "Are you a vet? Did you save Sue?"

He was already walking toward the barn. We caught up with him as he stared at Sue. Immediately she pushed her nose up, and Michael reached over. He laid his hand on her head, and she rolled her head so he would scratch her ear.

"She likes me!" Michael beamed to us. Mrs. Prinekles shook her head. Mr. Prinekles pulled me aside.

"We'd like to try Sue with us for the next week and see how it goes. Would you like to see where Sue is going?"

"Oh yes. I sure would."

We got Sue in the back of their Country Squire station wagon, and we were off. Driving into Dixon was a step back in time. There was one main road with small houses, each with a few acres. We pulled off the main road onto a dirt road that was lined with Sycamore trees and a white board fence running down the road on both sides. Mr. Prinekles pulled the station wagon up to a freshly painted barn with a corral.

"This is my home!" Michael told me. "This is Sue's home too, right Mom?"

Mrs. Prinekles was smiling. "Now, Michael we already discussed this. We're going to keep Sue for a while and see if Sue is happy here. You remember what we talked about?"

Michael was still smiling. "I know, Mom. Let's get Sue into her new home!"

We got Sue into the corral without any trouble, and Michael was soon feeding her some bananas. I knew then that Sue had a home. I'd be sure to tell Popeye that Sue was set up. I later took some flowers to Mrs. Prinekles at her office, and I thanked Dr. Dans for all his help.

Now, to get that starter in my truck.

The Preceptorship

Naked came I into the world, and naked must I go out.

Don Quixote

1972

I sat in my apartment staring at my stuffed two-headed calf and wondering where I was going to stay for the summer. I had no job prospects, little money, and had to be out of my apartment by the end of June.

I went by the Student Affairs Office to inquire about jobs on campus. The previous year I'd worked for the university in their summer Pig Project, and although it was interesting, I didn't wish to repeat the experience.

"Do you have any job openings for students this summer?"

The student coordinator, Miss Ruth, had a desk overflowing with papers. She turned to reach for a binder in the bookcase behind her, and as she pulled one binder out, three more tumbled to the ground, sprung open, and dispersed their contents across the floor and under her desk. "Oh sh...I mean oh shoot, oh shoot." She turned and looked back at me. "You didn't hear that!"

"Hear what?" I smiled at her.

She smiled back and opened the binder. "Well, there is an opening at the Primate Center cleaning cages." My classmate, Jim Paulson, had that job the year before and had told me all about cleaning those cages. That wasn't for me.

I shook my head. "I think I'll pass on that one. Anything at the Veterinary Clinic?"

"No, those jobs are all full-time positions, and we rarely have veterinary students employed there." She continued to leaf through her binder. She stopped and put her finger on one page. "Have you heard about the Preceptorship Programs?"

"The what?"

"They're jobs with veterinarians where you work at their clinics and stay with them, so you get free room and board."

"Is that like free room and board and no pay?"

She looked up at me. "You catch on quickly, don't you?"

"Could you tell me what you have?"

"There are three still available. One is in Los Angeles..."

I shook my head. "I'd like to stay in northern California, and I don't think I even have enough money to drive that far."

"Okay, there is another one in Riverside, and the last one is in Dublin."

"Where's Dublin?"

"You don't get out much do you? It's in the East Bay area, south Bay actually, below Concord."

"Where's Concord?"

She stopped and looked at me. "Do you know where San Francisco is?"

"Yes, I know where San Francisco is, but I've never been there."

There was distinct disbelief in her eyes. "Dublin is southeast of San Francisco."

"Maybe you could write down the telephone number, and I'll give them a call."

She was shaking her head. "That's not how it's done." She handed me a form. "Fill that out, and then I mail it to them with a copy of your transcript."

I took the form, went over to the side where there was a desk and sat down. I started to fill it out.

"You might want to type your answers."

"Oh, of course. I'll bring it back tomorrow."

She smiled, "That's a good idea. Also put down that you worked at the Pig Project last summer, and I'll give you a good reference. I know Larry."

I froze. "You know Mr. Daniels?" Larry Daniels was the head foreman of the University's Extension Division and had been my boss last summer. He had been the one to rescue me from the pig enclosure when I'd made the mistake of walking into the pen with their food rather than throwing it over the fence into the feeding bins, a mistake that I was lucky to have lived through and that I'd never forget. I thought Mr. Daniels would have a heart attack when he saw me getting stampeded by thirty-five hungry pigs.

"Larry is my husband. Don't worry, he told me you were the hardest working employee he had last summer and that you showed up for work every day on time— even the day after the pig incident." She laughed, and I felt embarrassed all over again.

That episode had followed me all year as news spread through the class about summer job experiences. It wasn't the best way to be recognized.

I tried to look serious. "Well, your husband saved my neck."

"Charlie, my husband thinks you're going to be a good vet. He knows about things like that. He's seen a lot of students go through, and he thinks highly of you." She put the binder back and turned back to me. "You fill that form out and bring it to me tomorrow. I'll put all the pieces together and get a letter from my husband to boot."

"Thank you." It wasn't much, but it was all I could say. The images of the pig stampede were becoming stronger, and I headed for the door.

· · · ·

A few days went by, and I was called to the Student Affairs Office. I had the summer job in Dublin with Drs. Nigel and Jamison. Half the summer I would stay with Dr. Nigel and the other half with Dr. Jamison. I'd work in their clinic six days a week, and they would pay me five dollars an hour—summer work, a free place to stay, and money. This was great; I said yes.

The school year ended. I'd made it through finals, I was elated when I got back my security deposit on my apartment, so with money in my pocket I packed up my belongings and headed for Dublin. I'd be doing a summer preceptorship at a real veterinary clinic; I was ready to learn.

It was arranged that my apartment stuff would be stored in Dr. Nigel's garage. As I pulled into the driveway a man in his late forties greeted me. He stood close to six feet, had blonde hair cut short, dark blue eyes and sported a golden tan. He looked healthy, maybe a runner. When he saw the two-headed calf he looked amused but not shocked.

"The famous two-headed calf! How'd you get that?"

"The pathology department was clearing out a storage room and had to let some specimens go. It was out in the hallway one day so I asked Dr. Polansky if I could have it. He said, 'Take it now before I change my mind,' so I loaded it into my truck and took it to my apartment between classes."

"Well, this sure brings back some memories of vet school for me. I can remember looking at it many times during my pathology rotation. I even showed it to my parents on their first visit to see me."

Dr. Nigel helped me get my things arranged, and I settled into his spare room. Dr. Nigel's first name was Dennis, and his wife's name was Toni. They had a son, Ted, who was also in college, attending a private one in Santa Barbara. Their son was staying in Santa Barbara for the summer since he had a job with a surf shop. I was to have Ted's room for my stay with them.

At the clinic, I helped hold pets for examinations, helped with treatments of pets, and watched surgeries. One morning, I was in charge of the treatments. Ron, one of the kennel staff, helped hold the patients as I took their temperatures, recorded them, and gave them their medications. I was trying to take Katie's temperature, a cat that was spayed the day before. She kept squirming, and it was difficult to hold the thermometer and her still at the same time. The thermometer was lubricated with KY-jelly, but Katie continued to move about and cry out. Finally Dr. Nigel came in.

"What's going on here, Charlie? Is Katie painful from her surgery? Is something wrong?"

"No, Dr. Nigel, it's just that she won't hold still. Every time I try to take her temperature she cries and jumps."

"Let me see." Dr. Nigel gently took Katie in his arms, and she began to purr. He lifted her tail and looked her over. Soon he was laughing. "Charlie, perhaps you should try taking her temperature rectally, instead of using her vulva."

Ron started laughing so hard I thought he would fall over. I must've been bright red because I sure felt hot. I held Katie as Dr. Nigel expertly took her temperature.

"One hundred degrees, incision looks good. You can take her back to her kennel, Ron."

I took Katie in my arms. "I'm sorry, Katie. Ron, I can take her back." I wanted to stay in the kennel room all day just so I wouldn't have to face Dr. Nigel and the rest of the staff; I felt so stupid.

The door opened and Dr. Nigel came in. "Charlie,

do you think you're the only one who makes mistakes?" I didn't answer him, just shrugged my shoulders. He continued, "It's one thing to make a mistake. It's worse not to admit it and far worse not to learn from it."

"Yeah, I guess."

"I bet you'll never make that mistake again." He put his hand on my shoulder, reminding me of how my dad would explain things to me.

"I won't."

"Come on, Charlie. There's lots to do today, and I need your help."

He walked out and the door closed behind him. I didn't know then, but I'd make a lot of mistakes in my career. Each time I was honest with my clients, and I learned from every mistake to make myself a better veterinarian. I've taken pride in never lying to a client and always reminding myself how I'd feel if I was the client.

I soon learned that the bedroom I was staying in had also been Jimmy's, the Nigel's seven year old male, neutered, Siamese cat. Jimmy wasn't happy with me moving in even though I left the bedroom door open for him.

The first week Jimmy would jump onto his bed, see me, hiss at me, and jump off. He did this for the first few weeks finally settling near the doorway. Soon he had ensconced himself onto Dr. Nigel's bed, much to Toni's displeasure. Oftentimes I'd hear a thud in the night followed by Jimmy's loud hissing. He'd come back to his own bedroom, only to see me in his bed, hiss some more and stealthily move off somewhere else.

About a month into my stay, Jimmy's stress level

became too much, and he decided one morning to mark his territory by urine spraying. Unfortunately, he chose Dr. Nigel's head. I awoke to "What the hell?" Jimmy hissing then followed by. "Jimmy, what're you doing? Get out of here!" Another loud thud and the sound of Jimmy's nails scurrying down the hallway.

Afterward, Jimmy slept in the garage until I moved to the Jamison's house. I felt sorry for Jimmy, but I was glad he didn't get the chance to use my head.

Some nights I'd sit in my room and read. On Sundays I'd make the rounds of the car lots; I've always liked cars. I'd drive into Dublin to the car lots and look at cars old and new. I especially liked the Corvettes, but there were also MGs, Jaguars, and Porsches to see. I could only dream of owning one.

The second half of the summer, I stayed with Dr. Jamison and his wife. Dr. Keith Jamison was almost as wide as he was tall. He had dark brown hair and penetrating eyes. His face had a perpetual smile, and he never seemed to be in a bad mood. He did the surgeries at this practice while Dr. Nigel saw most of the clients. I was amazed at how Dr. Jamison moved in the surgery room and by the dexterity of his hand motions in complicated surgeries. He did shoulder surgeries within forty-five minutes. At that time there were no board certified surgeons, but if there had been, Dr. Jamison would've been in their class. He made the surgeries seem so straightforward with his smooth and precise movements, I could tell this was his element, and he thoroughly enjoyed it.

He and his wife Joan had just moved into a very nice house, and my room was spacious. There were no children, so they went out often to eat. On the nights I was on my own I'd make my own meals trying to keep things neat and clean. Many times he'd take me with him on emergencies—in his brand new Corvette convertible!

"Charlie, I have to go back to the clinic for an emergency, and I think you'll want to see this one." Dr. Jamison had a big grin on his face. He didn't have to try very hard to persuade me into going with him since he always drove his Corvette. It was great to sit in that car.

"What's the emergency?"

"It's an older dog with a heart problem; the owner says he's coughing a lot tonight. I've seen it many times."

"So it has a lot of problems?"

Dr. Jamison was quiet.

"This dog is pretty sick?" I was trying my professional tone now.

Still silence.

"Okay, Dr. Jamison, what is it?"

He chuckled. "This dog, Petey, has had his usual problems with aging, but this particular owner just likes to have reassurance that she is doing all she can."

"And you think this cough is what?"

"Petey has congestive heart failure, and I've been adjusting his medication as his disease progresses, but that isn't why I asked you to come with me."

I was definitely interested now. "So why am I going?"

"Well, Charlie, when I was single this kind of client was a bonus of practice, but now that I'm married

I feel the need to have a little "insurance" when I see a client like this. Especially on emergencies when there is no office staff."

"And this would be, why...?"

"Charlie, every time this lady comes in she wears the briefest outfits. Each time she seems to get a little more daring. It's becoming uncomfortable."

Now I really was interested. *This profession just keeps sounding better and better,* I thought as we drove down to his clinic in his wonderful Corvette.

We pulled up to the clinic, and a gold Mercedes was sitting in the parking lot. As we got out of the Corvette, a tall woman stepped out of the Mercedes holding a small white bundle. She had on a long coat with a thick fur trim around the edge. She was wrapped up and didn't look at all risky to me. I was disappointed.

Dr. Jamison introduced her politely to me as Miss DeAngelo.

"Keith, thank you for coming out. Poor Petey is coughing something awful, and he can't rest. I just know he is suffering."

She placed Petey on the exam table, and he did look a little forlorn. His head was droopy, his tail hung down, and every so often he would hack and cough. I watched Dr. Jamison examine Petey. He had me listen to Petey's heart with his stethoscope.

"Can you hear that, Charlie? That is a grade three heart murmur. Petey is taking Lasix and Digoxin, but I think it is time to increase his dose of Lasix. I'm going to give him an injection right now."

Miss DeAngelo spoke up, "Keith, it's so warm in here I need to take this heavy coat off." And she did.

And she was wearing a bikini. And my mouth dropped open. And I had to grab my eyes before they fell to the floor. As I slowly recovered I stared over at Dr. Jamison. His back was turned to Miss DeAngelo, but I could see from the look on his face that he was telling me, *I told you so.*

• • • •

We got back into his Corvette and headed home in silence. Finally I recovered. "Does this happen very often?" I couldn't wait to graduate.

"If you mean Miss DeAngelo, yes." He looked over at me. "But there aren't many Miss DeAngelos so don't get your hopes up." He laughed, gunned the Corvette, and we were flying. *What a night.*

As we pulled into the garage he turned the engine off and opened the compartment between our seats. He held the Corvette's keys in his hand, and as he dropped them into the compartment, he smiled at me. "Charlie, this is where I keep the keys. If you ever want to take her for a drive just help yourself." He got out and bent to speak into the window. "See you in the morning."

I sat there for a while thinking about this night and then I opened the compartment and looked at those keys. I thought to myself that veterinary medicine just had to be the greatest profession there is.

The weeks went by quickly. Things got into a routine for me at the clinic, and I could do more and more without much supervision, but it was always interesting to watch the doctors examine and diagnose the pets. They would listen to the owners, and I could see that they were picking up clues from the animals as well. I imagined it as being a detective in search of the illness. I slept at night dreaming of the fantastic experiences that awaited me in practice.

One night, about a week before I was due back at school, Dr. Jamison came up to my room. "Charlie, Joan and I are going out to dinner with some friends. There is plenty to eat in the refrigerator just help yourself. We'll be back pretty late so I'll see you in the morning."

He was talking, but all I was hearing was, Charlie, this is where I keep the keys...I tried to look calm. "Sure, Dr. Jamison. Have a great time. See you in the morning."

I waited as he pulled Joan's Monte Carlo out of the garage. I heard the garage door shut. I watched them pull away down the road, around the corner, out of sight...

I grabbed my coat and ran down the stairs two at a time. I opened the door to the garage. There it was— the brand new, metallic green, 1972 Corvette convertible. I slid into the tan leather bucket seat. I opened the compartment. *No Keys!* Just a piece of folded up paper. It read, "Charlie, do you really think I would trust this baby to a twenty-three year old, testosterone loaded single guy? See you in the morning. Keith."

I still have that note.

First Impressions

But there's nothing half so sweet in life, As love's young dream.

-THOMAS MOORE

1973

When I arrived in Veterinary School, I became part of a special professional school. At that time, eighty-five students were in each class, and there were four classes in the school. During the fourth year (senior year), the students began seeing patients under the watchful eye of our professors. After three years of studies, books, laboratories, and exams we were allowed to be part of the real world of veterinary medicine.

As we went through the first, second, and third years of veterinary school, we would see the fourth year students in professional attire with their instruments hanging from their pockets and stethoscopes around their necks. They looked older, acted older—they looked like veterinarians!

George, my classmate and study partner, and I would sit looking out the window as we studied for exams. The two of us would talk about the opportunities awaiting us in the fourth year of veterinary school if we could just make it through the first three years. Were we thinking of diagnoses we would make? Were we thinking about the many and varied pets we would see? Maybe we were thinking about the surgeries we would actually be performing? Nope. We were thinking of the cute girls who came in with their pets. We could finally meet girls!

In those days, veterinary students studied dogs and cats, as well as large animals: horses, cows, pigs, and sheep. During the school year, we would rotate through all these fields of study. In the horse rotation, we would visit ranches, and part of the time we would work in the clinics at the veterinary school. The new barns were large with non-slip rubberized floors, two stations to examine horses, counters of medications, syringes, bandaging materials, horses, and the cute girls who came in with their horses. George and I couldn't wait to get to the horse rotation and into the clinics.

Now George and I were firm small animal students so we weren't in our best form with the livestock. We knew enough to run if a bull began stomping the ground with its feet, and we knew what the front and back of a horse looked like so we figured we could pull it off and impress the girls.

We'd hang out in the horse barn doing the easier treatments keeping our eyes open for a horse trailer pulling up to the clinic barn. When that happened we would take turns as to who got to *help* the equine clinician on staff.

George looked at me as a big, shiny Ford pickup pulled into the clinic grounds. It was pulling a horse trailer with matching paint. A woman with gray hair was driving, and a girl with long blond hair got out of the truck when it stopped.

George hesitated.

"Go ahead, George, its your turn," I encouraged him.

He positioned his stethoscope prominently and dusted down his coveralls. "Does my hair look okay?" He turned to face me.

I straightened his collar. "You'd better wipe off your boots just a bit but not too much," I helpfully added.

"Oh, man, do you see that?" George was watching as the girl led her horse out of the trailer and onto the asphalt in front of the clinic barn. "She's beautiful."

I laughed to him, "Yeah, and the girl looks pretty too."

"You know what I mean." George turned and marched off.

"Good luck, George."

I continued walking through the barn and checking the stalls, indicating my observations and checking treatment schedules on the appropriate animal records. There was a ewe with two lambs in one stall, a large boar in another stall, but in most of the stalls were horses.

I was cleaning out a stall when George returned. He was quiet.

"Well?" I couldn't take it any longer. "How did it go?"

"Charlie, do you know why there is a string tied to the thermometers?"

"My thermometer doesn't have a string on it," I observed. "It's brand new and still in its case." I had that clipped to one of my pockets along with my new pen. They looked real good.

George kicked at some straw. "You'd better tie a very long piece of string to that thermometer."

"What in the world for, George?" We had used thermometers, a smaller size I grant you, all during the last rotation in the small animal clinic. "None of my other thermometers have string on them."

George turned around and sat down on a bale of hay. He looked sad.

"What? What happened, George?"

"Well, I went into the clinic, and Dr. Roberts brought that horse into the barn. The girl was smiling at me and, man oh man, was she cute. Her name is Julie, and she came in with her aunt."

"So did you get a chance to talk with her, George?" That was when I noticed George's thermometer was not in his pocket.

"Charlie, it was awful. I listened to the horse's heart and recorded the heart rate. Then I went around to take its temperature. I picked up its tail and put my thermometer in, and Julie came up next to me. She smiled at me and asked me my name then all of a sudden my thermometer was gone."

"Gone?!" My imagination began to run with the complications.

George looked up, "Gone, Charlie, gone! Julie was watching me the whole time, and her eyes got real big, and she ran over to her aunt. I reached in as far as I could, but I couldn't find that thermometer. By this time Dr. Roberts came over, and I told him what had happen."

I was busy tying a piece of string onto my thermometer. "So what happened?"

"Nothing happened. Dr. Roberts said that it would just be passed when the next 'road apples' came out, then he laughed. He talked with Julie and her aunt and they began laughing. I just walked away."

"George, George, don't worry about it. Dr. Roberts said it was okay, and you'll never see those people again, so don't make yourself sick over it." George was watching me while I was tying the string onto my thermometer. I quickly put it away. "Come on; help me finish cleaning this stall."

After lunch we came back to the horse barn, and Dr. Roberts was busy working on another horse. This time a rugged-looking old cowboy was standing by and with him was a young girl. I looked over at George. "Oh no, Charlie! Not again. You go."

I positioned my stethoscope around my neck with it dangling in front of my coveralls. I made sure my string was tied securely to my thermometer. I smiled at George. "Watch this!"

"Good afternoon," I was smiling at the young girl. "How may I assist you, Dr. Roberts?"

Dr. Roberts looked at me as though I had come from outer space. He knew I was going into small animal medicine, and he would've rather had a large animal student helping him. "Try taking the temperature, Charlie." When I pulled my thermometer out with its new string attached, I could see he was smiling.

As I walked behind the horse, I was shaking the thermometer down and smiling at the young girl who was standing there watching me as my thermometer hit against my stethoscope and shattered into pieces. I stopped and looked down at the floor, holding in my hand a small piece of the thermometer firmly attached to the string. The young girl ran over to her dad, they both turned to look at me, broad smiles appeared. I looked up across the barn, and George was laughing hysterically. Dr. Roberts was shaking his head. Dejectedly, I excused myself and walked over to George.

"George, what do you say we get out of these coveralls and see what's happening up in the small animal clinics?" George put his hand on my shoulder as we walked back to the locker room to change.

"You know, Charlie, I think you have to be born into large animal medicine—it just can't be learned."

I smiled at him and handed him what was left of my thermometer. "Well, at least I didn't lose it."

We ran up the stairs to the small animal clinic.

My First Real Job

While we stop to think, we often miss our opportunity.

MAXIM 185

In May 1974; I was living in an apartment off campus, and I would be graduating veterinary school the following month. I had a yellow dining table with two vinyl matching chairs, a mattress on the floor, a few cooking utensils, and my stuffed, two-headed calf in a large display case on wheels.

I'd taken my last college loan advance in October, so money was becoming short. The last three months I'd been living on Colonel Saunders Giblets and cottage cheese. I was studying for the National Boards and State Boards and wondering what I'd do after graduation since I had no job prospects. One evening I got a telephone call.

"Hello, is this Charlie Freed?" It was an older man, sounding quite distinguished.

"Yes, this is Charlie Freed."

"Well, Mr. Freed, this is Dr. Irvine calling, and I understand you will be graduating veterinary school next month. I'm wondering if you would like to interview for a job opening I have?"

Who is this Dr. Irvine and how does he know me? "Dr. Irvine, thank you for calling, I am looking for a job."

"Well, why don't you come down and see what I'm offering? Would this Saturday work for you?"

At this point I would have agreed to anything to secure a job. My first job had come looking for me. I was excited.

"Yes, yes, Saturday would be fine. Where are you calling from?"

"I own the Irvine Veterinary Hospital in San Bruno. I would like to see you at one o'clock on Saturday afternoon, and I'll take you to lunch." He gave me the address and directions.

As he was talking, I took out my wallet and counted my money. Twenty-two dollars.

"About how far is San Bruno from U. C. Davis, Dr. Irvine?"

"It's about one hundred miles."

Gas was cheaper in those days, so I knew I could make it down to San Bruno and back to Davis with my twenty-two dollars. He gave me directions to his hospital.

"Thank you Dr. Irvine, I'll be there Saturday afternoon at one o'clock. Thank you for calling."

I found out later that Dr. Hollander, my neurology professor, had been a speaker at a veterinary meeting for the San Bruno Veterinary Association. I didn't realize he'd even noticed me in class, but he had told Dr. Irvine about me.

Saturday morning I filled up my gas tank and drove to San Bruno.

Dr. Irvine was about six foot five, thin, very tan, with silver hair and a lot of it. Glasses with thin gold rims sat on his angular nose and he was so clean shaven it was hard to tell he even had any facial hair. His clothing was impeccable—white long-sleeved shirt, a blue tie with faint red stripes, gray slacks, and on his feet, very large, shiny black wingtips. He took me to lunch, and I ordered a lot of food since it was the first good meal I'd had in three months.

"I notice that you are wearing jeans, Charlie, but if you accept my offer I require my doctors to dress like doctors—white shirt, tie, slacks, and a white lab coat."

"Uh, that would be fine, Dr. Irvine."

"Well then, what do you think, are you interested in the job?"

"Yes, sir, I am."

"And when could you start?"

"Well, I graduate on June 16, that's a Saturday. I could start the following Monday."

Dr. Irvine smiled. "I'm glad you're that eager, but why don't you start the following week?"

I had three days to be out of my apartment after graduation. "If it's just the same with you Dr. Irvine I'd like to start Monday."

At this point I was wondering where I'd stay since I had no money.

Dr. Irvine was quiet for a while as he watched me

devour my lunch. He cleared his throat. "Charlie, would you like an advance on your paycheck?"

"Well, Dr. Irvine, I have to tell you I haven't worn slacks for the last four years. I don't know where I'll stay, and I only have twelve dollars in my pocket."

He smiled and took out his checkbook and wrote a check. He then wrote a few lines on some notebook paper. "Here's an advance on your payroll. I'll figure out how to deduct it later, but for now I'm giving you enough for you to get some clothes and a place to stay." He gave me the check and note. "I know the owner of this apartment complex, and if you show him this note, he won't ask for a security deposit." He handed me a check for five hundred dollars. I was shocked. "Thank you Dr. Irvine. I'll go over there right after lunch."

So I cashed the check, secured an apartment and then went to J. C. Penney's in San Mateo to buy some clothes. I picked out three white shirts, one tie, and three pairs of slacks. Since I'm somewhat vertically challenged, I had to have the slacks shortened, and in those days Penney's had a person in their store to do that.

I went over to a small area where an older man with a bushy mustache, peppered white, wearing a red bow tie, brown vest, blue shirt and brown trousers was busy working. He turned as I approached.

"How may I help you, young man?" He had a tape measure around his neck hanging like a scarf, holding one end with his right hand. In his left hand was a piece of chalk.

"I have three pairs of pants that I need shortened."

"Very well, please step over to the changing room

and come out when you're ready. I'll have you stand over here." He pointed to a raised platform in the middle of the floor.

He measured, chalked and pinned the legs of my pants, and, one by one, they were put on a hanger with my name, my new address, but no telephone number.

"No telephone?"

"No, I am graduating from U. C. Davis next month, and I will be starting my first job with Dr. Irvine.

"Ah, you're a veterinarian? I know Dr. Irvine from Rotary. He's a good man."

"Well, I'm not a veterinarian yet, but I graduate next month."

He picked up a pair of my pants and sat down at his table.

"I'll have these ready for you by 4:00 p.m. today."

"Thank you. I will see you then."

• • • •

Graduation was great, with my mother and dad, sisters and brothers-in-law all attending. I moved my meager belongings to my apartment in San Mateo, getting a lot of looks as I drove down the freeway with the stuffed, two-headed calf in the back of my Ford pickup. My first week of practice went well and by Friday night I was tired and glad to be in my own apartment.

Since I had worn all three of my outfits in one week I headed down to the laundry room to get them washed and dried, ready for another week of work. I knew from college never to leave clothes in a dryer unattended, but as the washer was going I went across the street to an all night donut chop for a cup of coffee and a donut. When I returned the washer lid was up.

I stared down into the empty washer. *Empty Washer!* I went to the other two washers hoping I'd forgotten which one I'd used, but they were empty too. My new clothes were gone! Someone had actually taken them from the washing machine. I stood there for a few minutes with my hands on the empty washer looking down into the dark void. I had no extra money for more clothes.

Monday morning I showed up for work in cleaned, washed, ironed and creased jeans. An old frayed shirt, with my tie on. My boss was not pleased.

"Charlie where are your slacks, your white shirt!" My second week of work and already I'm a disappointment.

I explained to Dr. Irvine what had happened and again watched him write a check to me that would be deducted from my future pay. At this point, I realized my paycheck was quickly dwindling. Not quite what I'd imagined veterinary medicine would be.

Once again I stood in J. C. Penney's.

"What is this?" The old man was waving his finger at me. "You must really like these pants; didn't I just do some for you?"

When I explained what had happened, a very serious expression came to his face. "You've paid again for these pants?"

"Yes, sir."

"Then there'll be no charge for the alterations. I do them for free for you. I know what it's like to start out with nothing, but you'll see, things will get better." He busied himself with measuring, chalking and pinning again, mumbling all the time. When he was done he looked up at me. "You work tomorrow?"

"Yes, sir."

"You come by here before five o'clock today, and one pair will be ready for you. I'll start right now."

He stood up. I put my hand out, and he grasped it.

"I can't begin to thank you. I've already borrowed two times on my paycheck."

"That is fine, young man, because some day you'll help someone else."

He was right. Over the years I've passed his kindness on to others I've met. If they tell me how thankful they are, I repeat his words to 'help someone else' when they can. It's been thirty-four years, and I still remember that man as clearly as if it was yesterday.

Kindness lives forever.

Decisions

Thursday 11:30 *a.m.: DeAgrea dog, Taffy, euthanasia.*

During my first few months working at the veterinary hospital, Dr. Irvine gave me cases such as nail trims, vaccinations, and euthanasias. He thought those would be safe procedures for me. As he said, "The first two you can't hurt, and the last one doesn't matter." I watched the other doctors do surgery and once in a while one would let me close an incision for him, but after months of feeling under-appreciated for all my learning, I felt I had to make a change to show my boss what I was capable of doing. Why, I'd just graduated from a prestigious veterinary college. I knew all there was to know about pheochromocytomas, hyper- and hypo-adrenal corticism, and malignant hyperthermia. I needed to be in that exam room and diagnosing!

Then that fateful day arrived.

I opened the client record to read the receptionist's note, "Euthanasia, poodle, Taffy." I decided today would be different!

I walked into the exam room confidently, as only a new graduate can. My tie was straight, my exam coat white and pressed and my stethoscope hung snugly around my neck. On the exam table lay Taffy. A black miniature poodle, in dire need of veterinary attention! She was panting heavily, with a mouth odor that cried out, *Diabetes! Ketones! Dentistry!* Next to Taffy stood a nice looking young woman whose face was streaked with tears, her eyelids red and swollen. By the door sat an older lady looking slightly bored and disinterested. "Ahem." I gazed at Taffy seriously. The panting seemed to be increasing, and the mouth odor was almost more than I could bear as I leaned in closer. "I'm sorry that euthanasia has to be considered today." I began, holding my stethoscope to the left side of Taffy's chest and hearing a loud heart murmur. "You know there have been quite a few advances in veterinary medicine." At this, the young woman stopped crying and looked at me with hope, so I attempted a smile on her behalf. Taffy's eyes seemed to be enlarging in front of mine. "We could do an EKG, chest radiographs, maybe draw a blood sample..." Just then Taffy made a wretched noise. The young woman jumped back from the table. All was still. Taffy's panting had stopped; she lay motionless.

My mouth felt dry, and my tongue felt swollen. I looked up at the young woman who again was crying and gently stroking the recently deceased. Quietly, clearly, from the direction of the old lady the following words rang into my ears, "It looks like the old girl beat you, Doc."

The old lady and young woman embraced and walked out of the exam room. Standing there, looking down at Taffy, I opened the record and recorded, "pet died before euthanasia could be performed," and stepped into the hallway. Soon Dr. Irvine walked up to me with a quizzing look, "Why didn't you charge for the euthanasia?" I mumbled something and picked up the next chart. The note on the front said, "Nail trim, miniature Doxie, *be careful.*"

A Safe Place

Monday 11:00 a.m.: Ritwoods' dog, Max, coughing.

The next day was going well, and at 11:00 a.m. one of my favorite patients would be coming in, Max and his wonderful owners the Ritwoods. Max was a Sheltie mix whose luxurious coat must have taken hours of daily brushing. He looked and acted regal and was a joy to work with. Max would strut into the reception area and sit patiently at his owner's side. He seemed so intelligent that I used to look at him when I was talking to the Ritwoods because he appeared to understand what I was saying. After a procedure was done, he would often turn to lick my hand without even an undignified sniff at my jacket pocket where I carried treats for lesser dogs.

I looked at Max's file before I walked into the exam room. He was coming in for coughing. Since Max was never boarded at a kennel, a simple diagnosis of "kennel cough" was unlikely. Today Max sat quietly in the exam room, looking tired and weak. My greeting to the Ritwoods was harder to do; I sensed a smile and a cheerful handshake was out of place. The look of concern on the Ritwoods' faces made me all the more worried.

"It's nice to see you today, but I'm sorry Max isn't feeling well. Can you tell me what you've noticed?"

There was a silence for a few seconds as they looked at each other and then Mrs. Ritwood spoke up. "Max started to cough about a month ago. It was so infrequent that we really didn't know he was having a problem. He was eating well and still wanted to go for his walks." At this point, she stopped talking, and I noticed her hand just touching her husband's. He gave it a quick squeeze and she went on. "In the last few days it seems Max can't get comfortable. He is up and down all night and doesn't want to go on his walks. The last two days he hasn't been hungry, and his cough keeps him up at night and us too."

As she was talking, I was looking Max over. I put my stethoscope to his chest and could hear the moist rales and the left mitral murmur. It didn't sound encouraging, and I tried to find the right words to use. "It appears that Max has a heart murmur, and fluid is building up in his lungs." They didn't say anything waiting for me to continue, but I sensed they already knew what I'd say. "I think Max should stay with me for awhile so I can take some radiographs of his chest and draw a blood sample." They readily agreed.

"I'll see you this afternoon Mr. and Mrs. Ritwood. I think there will be something I can do for old Max."

"Thank you, Dr. Freed. We'll check with Shirley and see what time is best to come back."

It turned out that Max did indeed have an enlarged

heart and probably did have congestive heart failure, but what I wasn't prepared for were the many 'coin' lesions throughout his chest that I had learned in veterinary school was a sign of metastatic cancer. I remember going to lunch that day wondering what I'd tell the Ritwoods when they came back that afternoon to pick up Max. I found I didn't have any appetite so I soon headed back to the veterinary clinic to prepare for the afternoon appointments.

When the Ritwoods came back for Max, it wasn't easy to tell them that their beloved friend had more than heart failure to deal with. There were the usual questions on how long would he live, was he in pain, and when would they know if he would have to be put to sleep. It was odd because I was the one who was crying.

Max went home on digoxin, lasix, and prednisolone, and he actually seemed to improve over the next few days. However, I knew in time he'd decline, and I'd get that call for euthanasia. Weeks turned into months, and when I did get the call from the Ritwoods, I couldn't believe that three months had gone by. I picked up the telephone ready to give the Ritwoods my best.

"Hello, Mrs. Ritwood?"

"Yes, hello, Dr. Freed," she seemed better composed than I thought she'd be. "I wanted to let you know that Max passed away last night."

"Oh, Mrs. Ritwood I'm so sorry. He was such a beautiful pet, and I really enjoyed seeing him."

"I want you to know that Max was more comfortable, and he was coughing less. His appetite slowly went down, but even yesterday he ate some treats that my husband gave him at lunch time." Before I could respond, she continued. "Last night we heard Max leave our bedroom, where he always slept. We thought he went down to get a drink of water and really didn't think much about it. This morning when we woke up and didn't see Max by our bed, we knew something was wrong. My husband went down to the kitchen, but Max wasn't there. He started to go out to the living room, but then he noticed that the door to the basement was open. When he went down to the basement he found Max laying on the floor. It was obvious that Max had tried to get something off the shelf because towels were on the floor and the mop and broom were knocked off their holders. He found Max lying on the floor as if he was sleeping, with his head resting on his old puppy bed; he'd knocked it off the shelf. Why we never got rid of that bed, I don't know, but my husband had put it up on the shelf with some extra towels. I guess Max wanted to be in his old bed."

After Mrs. Ritwood hung up, I sat there with the picture in my mind of Max, lying by his little puppy bed. Although I worked the rest of the day, I wasn't up to it. I just kept thinking that in Max's last hours, when he knew things were getting worse, he went in search of the one place he'd felt safe as a puppy.

Define "Emergency"

Monday 8:30 p.m.: Peterson's dog, Buddy, panting.

That night I was glad to get back to my apartment; it'd been a long day. I sat down on the sofa and through the sliding glass doors I could see the S. F. Airport and watch the planes taking off and landing, people going on trips. The first months of practice had been nothing like I'd imagined. There were so many things I didn't know. I was thankful that I was working with four other veterinarians so I could frequently ask questions, but it was the technicians who really pulled me through those first months. They knew so much. One technician, Riley Beachamps, had been with this veterinary clinic for eleven years. His experience was invaluable to me, and I was grateful for his insights on many cases.

I changed my clothes and headed over to the bowling alley across El Camino. There was a café there, and I had a hamburger and fries while I watched the people bowl. When I got back to my apartment the telephone was ringing. I was on call that night for emergencies. I was scared stiff since I was finding out every day that I didn't know as much as I thought I did when I graduated, so I'd arranged with Riley that I could call him if I ever needed help.

"Hello?"

"Is this Dr. Freed?"

"Yes."

"Dr. Freed, this is the answering service, and we have an emergency call for you."

"Okay put them through. Hello, this is Dr. Freed."

"Hello, Dr. Freed. It's our dog, Buddy."

"Yes."

"Well, we got home from work, and he is panting and panting. It's like he can't catch his breath. We need to bring him in right away."

"Okay that's fine, but tell me, can you look at his gums and see if they are pink?" There was some silence for a while.

"Yes, Dr. Freed, Buddy's gums are nice and pink."

"That's good. What is Buddy doing right now?"

"Well, he is sitting looking up at us and panting."

"And this isn't usual for him when you come home from work?"

"Oh no, Dr. Freed, he runs around like crazy and then he goes into the kitchen and waits for his dinner."

"Have you fed him tonight?"

"No, we didn't because he was panting so much."

I could tell there was no way out of this. I was tired from working all day, but it looked like I'd have to go back and see Buddy. I wrote down their name and telephone number. "Okay, Mr. Peterson, I can meet you at the hospital within twenty minutes."

"Thank you, Dr. Freed, we are on our way."

I drove down to the hospital feeling pretty sleepy and thinking I should stop and get some coffee, but I didn't want to be late. I always try to beat the clients to the hospital so I have time to get things ready. I got to the hospital, found their record, turned on the exam room light and waited.

And waited. After awhile I went out to the reception desk where I could sit down and look right at the front door. And waited.

I woke up. It was 11:30 p.m.! I'd fallen asleep at the desk! Had I missed the Petersons? Had they come to the hospital and knocked on the door, and I didn't hear them? Had Buddy died? I was beginning to feel nauseous. How could I've fallen asleep and missed this emergency? What could they possibly think, coming down and not finding me ready to help? What a failure. I couldn't stand the thought that something terrible had happened to Buddy. It was all my fault. I called the San Mateo Emergency clinic and asked them if they'd seen the Petersons but they hadn't. All I could think was Buddy had died and all because I'd fallen asleep. I just had to call the Petersons and apologize to them.

"Hello."

"Mr. Peterson?"

"Yes, who is this?"

"Mr. Peterson this is Dr. Freed. Is Buddy Okay?"

"Of course Buddy is fine. We fed him his dinner, and he's just fine. We're just getting ready to go to bed."

"You mean you didn't go down to the hospital?"

"No, we didn't see any reason to. Once we fed Buddy he stopped panting, and he's been sleeping here all night while we watched TV. But thank you for calling." He hung up.

I couldn't believe I'd spent the night sleeping at the receptionist's desk while they watched TV. Why didn't they call me? I would never know. But I would soon find out odder things would happen.

Miss Miranda and the Snake

Friday 10:30 p.m.: Ms. Miranda's boa, Clancey, lethargic.

I was working the 6:00 p.m. to 6:00 a.m. shift at the San Mateo Emergency Clinic one night. After graduating from Veterinary School, I owed a lot of money in student loans, so when I could, I'd pick up a night's work at the emergency clinic and use the extra money to help pay off my loans. This evening the receptionist came back to the room that the vets used between cases. I was sitting on the narrow bed and watching an old movie on a small, fuzzy-screen TV.

"Dr. Freed, do you know anything about boa constrictors?"

"Not much Lindy. I know what I learned in veterinary school, but I really haven't treated any."

Lindy went over to the small library and pulled down a book. "This is the book that Dr. Reedy uses. I think you better look at this. You're going to see a nine foot boa in about thirty minutes."

The book was Dr. Fredric Frye's *Medicine and Hus-*

bandry of Captive Reptiles. I quickly looked up boas. "Do you know why it's coming in, Lindy?"

She turned and smiled at me. "It's lethargic and it has a show tonight."

I let that sink in a minute. "A show?"

"Yep, the lady said she was headed to work, and her boa was lethargic, and she needs it peppy for her act."

"You're joking me aren't you, Lindy?"

She turned and headed down the hall. "Thirty minutes, Doc."

I was frantic. I knew next to nothing about snakes. I was reading like crazy when Lindy called.

I closed the book and walked into the exam room. Sure enough, there was a very large boa constrictor and a very tall lovely lady in full makeup and beneath her tiny coat, were very long, beautiful legs ending in very long black high heels.

"Good evening." Looking at the record before me, "Uh, Miss Miranda. Clancey is not himself?"

"He's just laying there, Doc." She had Clancey around her neck, and he was just lying there draped across her breasts, he nearly reached to her knees. I had no idea what to do. I reached out and helped her unwrap Clancey from under her long auburn curls.

"Has he eaten today?"

"Oh no, Doc. I feed him once every three weeks and never before our act."

Well, there went that diagnosis. I tried to remember what else Dr. Frye had written. I looked at Clancey's eyes, his mouth, listened to his heart, felt over his scales, checking for mites. I didn't find anything. "Well, I don't see anything obvious, Miss Miranda but I'll start him on an antibiotic, and I hope that will make him feel better. Be sure to check with your regular veterinarian in the morning." I gave Clancey an injection of antibiotic and a vitamin injection. He didn't seem to mind, even though my hand was shaking just a little.

"When do you go on?"

"Well, I still have to drive into San Francisco so it will be about another hour before our show. What do you think, Doc?"

"I have to tell you that I'm not sure what is wrong. The injections I gave won't cause any harm, but I don't know how much improvement you'll see in an hour. When you get to the theater, can you wrap him in a heating blanket and turn it on the lowest setting."

"Gee, Doc I don't have one. Do you really think that's necessary?"

I saw Lindy go down the hall and come back with a blanket in a bag. "Here you go, Miss Miranda. You can borrow this and bring it back tomorrow night. We open at 6:00 p.m."

I looked at Lindy. "Thanks, Lindy." I turned back to my client. "Getting Clancey's body temperature up should make him feel better, but be sure to use the lowest setting."

"Thank you, Doc. And you, Lindy. I'll bring this back tomorrow."

She went to the lobby. I watched her pay her bill and then walk out with long graceful strides. I went back to my room to find only a sheet on the bed. Just then Lindy walked in.

"So that's where the blanket came from. Thanks

a lot, Lindy. You'd better turn the thermostat up tonight."

Lindy was smiling. "Don't worry, Doc, I don't think you'll have much time to sleep. We have two basset hounds coming in that just ate some snail bait."

• • • •

A few nights later I found myself working at the emergency clinic again.

"Hey, Doc, good to see you." Lindy was smiling. "Miss Miranda brought that blanket back and told me you missed a good show. Clancey did fine." Lindy handed me an envelope. "I couldn't wait to see you again. She left this for you, and we all want to know what's inside."

I took the envelope and looked at the seal. "I'm surprised you guys didn't already steam it open." I pulled out a nice card on which Miss Miranda had written a very warm thank you note and inside were two tickets to her show at the Mitchell Brothers' Theater in San Francisco. I handed the card and tickets over to Lindy. "Say, Lindy, what are you doing tomorrow night?"

Sweet Little Thing

Sunday 11:00 p.m.: Bower's dog, Missy, torn feet.

About a month later I was working at the emergency clinic when I heard a commotion in the lobby. I decided to wait for Lindy. It wasn't long before she came running down the hall.

"Doc, this is bad. Real bad." Lindy had been working here for over three years. If she thought this was bad, she had my heart pounding too.

"What is it, Lindy?"

"I've got a couple out there with their Chihuahua. It caught its feet in the escalator at the airport, and there's blood everywhere."

We got them into the exam room, and I looked down at the tiny dog on the table in front of me. The worried parents were a Mr. and Mrs. Bower. They had gone to meet some friends at the airport. Missy, their Chihuahua, had four badly torn and bleeding feet. It was difficult to tell what was left, but her feet looked terrible, and the Bowers were hysterical.

"Mr. and Mrs. Bower, Lindy and I are going to take Missy to the treatment area. We're going to anesthetize her and clean and examine her feet. Can you wait in the lobby for us?"

They just looked at us in shock. Lindy took them out to the lobby and got them some coffee and then came back to help me.

We anesthetized Missy and thoroughly cleaned her feet. Her right front foot was crushed, but we aligned it and wrapped it in an antibiotic bandage. On her left front foot, I had to amputate the dewclaw and second toe. I sutured the torn skin, and after cleaning it put it also in an antibiotic bandage. The rear feet were not as bad, but there were cuts that needed to be sutured and the large pads on both feet had been torn off so there was nothing there to suture. Those areas would have to heal by granulation, so all we could do was clean and bandage them. We started intravenous fluids and added antibiotics to the fluids. We then set Missy up in a heated kennel.

I finally went out to the lobby to explain things: "Well, Missy is resting well. She has lost two toes..."

They both started to cry. "Will we have to put her to sleep?"

"Oh no. That's not at all necessary. She..."

"Will she be able to walk? Will she lose her feet?" She can't walk without feet!"

"Now Mr. and Mrs. Bower, please let me explain. I think Missy is going to do very well. Lindy and I have cleaned and sutured her wounds. She can manage quite well without two toes. What she will need is to have her bandages changed by a veterinarian every five days until they've healed. This will take many weeks. She will also need to be on antibiotics the whole time."

They seemed relieved. "We can do that, Doctor. We love Missy. She is just the sweetest thing. We'd do anything for her. When can she go home?"

"I think she should stay here tonight so I can keep an eye on her and make sure her temperature is normal. I also want to check her bandages in the morning and give her another injection of antibiotic. Why don't you check with Lindy for the best time tomorrow?"

"Thank you, Doctor. We're so grateful. We thought you were going to tell us to put her to sleep."

"I think she'll do fine. Don't forget you'll need to have those bandages changed every five days."

"We will, Doctor; we will."

As they left, I noticed that they'd been dressed to meet their friends at the airport, Mr. Bower had on nice slacks and a wool jacket, his wife wore a fashionable skirt, with matching shoes and purse. Unfortunately, they were now both covered in blood.

Later that night, I went to check on Missy. I opened her kennel door, and she went from sleeping to attacking me in seconds. I barely got my hand out before she had time to clamp her teeth into it. "Holy Cow!" I had to disagree with the Bowers, Missy was *not* the sweetest thing!

Lindy heard me and came in. "What's up?"

"Well, I just wanted to check Missy out, take her temperature, check her gums, but she went crazy."

"Oh, Doc, she's just used to a woman's touch. I'll get her out for you." Lindy went up to Missy's kennel. "Hi there, little girl, let's take a look at you." I could see Missy's tail wagging. Lindy opened the kennel door and then shut it so fast it vibrated the whole row of kennels. "Good God! She almost got me! That little..."

"That sweet little thing, that's used to a woman's touch?"

Lindy whirled around at me, and by the look she gave me, I knew to keep my mouth shut. "She is something else!"

"You know, Lindy, that's what I like about working here at the emergency clinic. I'll never see that little dog again, and some other poor vet is going to have to risk his life to change her bandages every five days."

Lindy smiled at me. Yep, Doc, she's gone tomorrow at six a.m., and I won't have to see her again either. I think I'll order some pizza."

"Good idea, Lindy. Let me know when it comes and I'll pay for it." I headed back to the vets' room to watch some TV.

• • • •

The next week I was working at my full time job at the Irvine Veterinary Hospital in San Bruno when I heard a spirited conversation in the lobby.

"So, we called all the veterinary hospitals in San Mateo but no Dr. Freed. Then we started to call the veterinary hospitals in San Bruno and on the third call we found our Dr. Freed!"

I heard Shirley, the receptionist say, "Yes, Dr. Freed does work here."

I suddenly recognized the voices. How could this be happening to me?

"So we need to have Missy's bandages changed. Dr.

Freed was so kind and thoughtful we just couldn't trust our Missy to anyone else."

The Bowers and their vicious little Chihuahua! The door to my exam room opened, and Shirley came in. She was smiling.

"So Doctor Wonderful, you certainly impressed the Bowers. They have Missy outside for you to see. I guess her bandages need to be changed."

I took the chart from Shirley and saw a copy of my discharge instructions on top.

"She sure looks cute with those little bandages on her feet."

I gave Shirley a cold stare. "Well, she's not cute!"

"I'll tell the Bowers it'll just be a minute."

Thus began six weeks of Hell every five days. Missy took every available opportunity to bite me. But in spite of her disposition, her feet did heal well and soon she was walking with hardly a limp.

"Thank You, Dr. Freed. You're the best!" The Bowers praised me on their last visit with Missy.

I walked down the hall mumbling to myself, "...and the most stupid." I went into the bathroom to apply fresh Band-Aids to my fingers.

Rudy, Rudy, Rudy

Wednesday 2:00 p.m.: Lucy's dog, Rudy, bleeding from mouth.

The morning had been a long one, and I'd admitted enough animals that needed procedures to guarantee another no-lunch-hour day. We had seen appointments from 8:30 a.m. to 1:00 p.m. and, in addition, had managed to work in two emergencies: a Miniature Schnauzer with pancreatitis and a Golden Retriever with a cut footpad.

"Lucy, this has been a busy morning."

Lucy was washing her hands, "Doc, I think I'll run home for lunch."

"Sure, Lucy. I'll get Pam to help me. Go get some rest because it looks like a busy afternoon."

"See you in about an hour, Doc." Lucy hung up her smock and went out the side door.

I finished writing up the morning records and had Pam fill some prescriptions. We were getting ready to anesthetize Stormy, the Golden Retriever, when all of a sudden Lucy ran into the clinic carrying her Dober-man, Rudy. There was a lot of blood on Lucy's blouse.

"Doc, Rudy is bleeding from his mouth, I don't know what he's done." Lucy's alarm and the site of the blood got my adrenalin going.

"Okay, Lucy, lets look him over. Would you help us, Pam?" I knew how upsetting it was for employees to work on their own pet, and I planned to have Pam take over. We put Rudy on the treatment table; he was gagging every few minutes. There was dried blood all over his face, but I didn't see any active bleeding. I was worried he had something caught in his throat. "Lucy can you think of anything that Rudy could have swal-lowed and cut himself with?"

"Gee, Doc, I can't think of anything that could harm him."

Lucy was shaking; it was time for Pam to take over. "Lucy, why don't you go home and look around, maybe you can find some clues for us."

"Thanks, Doc, I really need to get the blood cleaned up. It's all over my house."

"Go ahead, Lucy. Pam and I will take care of Rudy. Go home and try to get some lunch too."

Pam was holding Rudy who was gagging even more now. I was getting ready to sedate him to exam his mouth when all of a sudden he vomited a lot of blood clots. What Pam and I saw made us stand still.

"Doc?"

"Hang on, Pam; I've got some phone calls to make!"

• • • •

Lucy was just walking into her kitchen when the telephone began ringing. She automatically rushed to answer it.

"Hello?"

"Lucy, this is Dr. Freed. Get out of the your house right this minute! Don't ask any questions just do it right now! *Right Now!*"

As Lucy left her house she could hear sirens in the distance. Within minutes two police cars drove up, one into her driveway and the other parked across the street.

"Lucy Lawrence?" The first officer asked.

"Yes, I'm Lucy. What is it officer? What's wrong?"

"Miss, we have reason to believe you have a burglar on your premises. Please go over to Officer McIntire across the street." His nametag identified him as Officer Durning.

Officer Durning and his partner entered the house. It wasn't long before they led a man out of the house holding a blood soaked towel over his hand. They put him into the patrol car; it backed out of the driveway and headed down the road with the siren blaring. Officer Durning walked across the street to them. "Found him in the bedroom closet, Dan." Turning to Lucy he continued, "I'm afraid there's a lot of blood in there, miss."

Lucy was confused. "Did he hurt Rudy? Is that how you knew?"

Officer Durning smiled, "No Miss, Rudy is going to be just fine. We got a call from a Dr. Freed at the

Irvine Veterinary Hospital. He told us that Rudy had come in with a lot of blood around his mouth and later vomited up a *human finger*. He told me he had already called you and told you to get out of your house."

"Rudy is okay?"

"Rudy is fine, but that guy is on is way to the hospital. You've got a true protector there, miss."

Lucy was sitting on the curb. "I've never seen Rudy even growl at another dog or person, but I guess he knew that man wasn't supposed to be in our house."

"Well, we'd better go down to the hospital. Is there any thing else we can do for you?"

Lucy stood up. "No, but thank you. Thank you very much." She shook their hands. Officer Durning handed her a piece of paper and his card.

"If you need anything you can contact me and use this number to identify the case. Oh and Dr. Freed said to take the afternoon off."

Lucy seemed relieved and smiled at the officers. "I'm going to clean myself up and then I'm going down to give Rudy a bath and a lot of love."

Dan looked over. "Would you like us to call your husband?"

Lucy smiled, "No. I'm not married."

Dan was grinning as he reached into his pocket and gave Lucy his card. "If I can be of any help just call me. Would you mind if I checked in later to see how you and Rudy are doing?"

Lucy looked at Dan's card and back at Dan, "That would be nice."

"Good luck, Lucy, and I'll call you later."

"Good-bye, Dan." As Lucy walked up her driveway, she was smiling and thought to herself, *and thank you Rudy.*

Time To Move On

And Life is never the same again.

-PHANTASTES

I'd learned a lot during my years working at the Irvine Veterinary Hospital and especially the times working at the San Mateo Emergency Clinic, but as the years went by, I was feeling stressed by the fast pace. I'd see so many clients a day that I often didn't have time to work up my cases until after work. I guess I was no different than other veterinarians of my time in that we all wanted to some day own a veterinary hospital.

My commute to work was becoming longer due to the traffic congestion, and I was tired of breathing air that felt like second hand smoke. It was time to branch out. I think the final decision was made one day when I watched my half-hour lunch disappear as I tried to get across the busy El Camino and into the Tanforan Shopping Center. I felt like I was constantly running.

My boss must've noticed my anxiety because one day he called me aside.

"Charlie, are you doing all right? You seem preoccupied. Is something wrong?"

I brushed my hair out of my face and took a deep breath. "Dr. Irvine, I'm thinking of moving out of the city."

"Charlie, I've talked with Drs. Lambson and Gyles, and we're considering offering you a partnership. Would you be interested in that?"

I was speechless. The Irvine Veterinary Hospital was one of the more progressive hospitals in the area. I admired my colleagues and felt like I was learning from them everyday. I never thought of myself in their category, certainly not a peer. To be offered a partnership was quite a compliment.

"Dr. Irvine, that's something I never considered."

"Well, would it change your idea of leaving?"

"Could you give me two weeks to think this over? I just had it in my mind it was time to move on, but this certainly gives me something to think about."

"I don't have to tell you that you would be getting a big jump in salary, in addition to medical and dental benefits. I hope you'll think this over, Charlie."

"Thank you, Dr. Irvine. I will. I'll let you know within the next two weeks."

"Charlie, if you would like to sit down with us I can arrange that."

"Thank you, I'll let you know."

Later that evening, I sat in my apartment staring again at the advertisement from a Veterinary Journal that I had clipped out a month ago:

Veterinary Clinic in Mendocino County, CA, for sale. Pastoral setting, open fields, friends for clients. Practice veterinary medicine on a personal level. Call Dr. Robert T. Davison at 707-555-5632.

Maybe I'd go up and see what it looked like and how much they wanted. I hoped that being a veterinarian would help me get a loan. I called the number and set up a day to see Dr. Davison and his clinic.

• • • •

Driving north down the Ridgewood Grade that Saturday in June 1978, was nothing short of a life changing experience. Pine trees and oaks surrounded me, rolling hills of open space, and as I drove down toward Willits, this beautiful valley stretched out before me. No freeways, no traffic jams, no stoplights, no smog. The sky was a crystal blue, the air felt clean. I found myself smiling as I drove into Willits.

Dr. Robert T. Davison, also a graduate of the U. C. Davis Veterinary School, owned the Redwood Veterinary Clinic. The clinic was a converted mobile home, and although it looked stark, the setting was great. Green pastures, an old two story barn and a stream running just to the north of the hospital. I pulled off the main road onto a dirt driveway that led up to the hospital.

By the barn were three horses grazing in the field. Six sheep were off in the distance, their white bodies standing out against the green grass. I already felt peaceful. I got out of my truck as a rancher brought two Border Collies out of the hospital and loaded them into the back of his truck. The hospital door was still open so I walked in.

To my right was a desk where a heavyset woman with a welcoming smile commanded the post.

"Hi. What can I do for you?"

"Hello. I'm Charlie Freed, and I have an appointment with Dr. Davison."

"Have you come about his ad to sell the hospital?"

"Well, I wanted to see what Willits looked like and maybe see what was being offered."

"Bobby, I mean Dr. Davison, wants to sell the small animal part of this practice and move the livestock part to his ranch. My name's Rachel. I've been with Dr. Davison since he started this clinic." She came around the desk. "Let me show you around while we're waiting for Doc."

The clinic was small, but well organized with one exam room, a surgery room, kennel area, inventory area, and lobby. "How long has the clinic been here?"

"Well, Doc has been in town since 1972. At first he lived right here. This was his home, and he did mainly ranch calls. As the practice built up, the small animal work increased, and by that time, Doc was able to buy a ranch just outside of town. That was 1976."

As we came back to the lobby a very tall, wiry man walked in. A typical cowboy type with brown, beaten up boots, faded Levis with a large silver buckle, a worn out green and black plaid shirt and a cowboy hat that looked like it had taken a few stompings.

"Doc, this is Charlie Freed."

I was hoping my shock didn't show on my face. He put out his large, calloused hand and shook mine. "Well, Charlie, it's nice to meet you. You're a city boy?"

Man was I a city boy! Here was Dr. Davison looking as if he had just gotten off a horse, and I was standing there in my black slacks and shiny shoes; I was definitely a city boy.

"I've been living in San Mateo and working in a four doctor practice in San Bruno."

Dr. Davison took his hat off and tossed it on the desk. His hair was thick, sandy and a little long. He combed it back from his forehead with his hand. "So, did you see the clinic?"

"Yes, Rachel gave me the tour."

"Well then, what do you think?"

We went out to lunch and discussed the money situation. Dr. Davison was selling the business and would rent the building to me. After lunch I went to the Bank of Willits to see about getting a loan. As I drove down Highway 101, Willits' Main Street, I marveled at the different types of people I saw. People dressed in business suits, cowboys and cowgirls riding horses right in the downtown, hippies wearing tie-dyed Tee shirts, and kids darting in and out of traffic on bicycles.

I went into the Bank of Willits and was introduced to one of the loan officers. His name was Mr. Garner.

"So, you've just graduated from veterinary school, Dr. Freed?"

"No, Mr. Garner. I graduated in 1974, and I have been working full time ever since at the Irvine Veterinary Hospital in San Bruno. I have managed to pay off my student loans by working extra at the San Mateo Emergency Clinic. I have five thousand dollars saved up."

"Let's see. Dr. Davison wants forty thousand dollars for his veterinary business. Do you think that's a good price?"

"Mr. Garner, I don't really know. This is the only place I've looked at, but this valley is beautiful, and I sure would like to leave the city."

"Are you from the country?"

"No, I grew up in Ventura, southern California, but the last few years I've been living in the bay area, working in San Bruno and San Mateo. I just don't think living in the city is what I want to do."

He busied himself with his calculator and looked through some books on his desk. He looked up at me. "These papers from Dr. Davison show a steady profit. I'll tell you what I can do, if you can pay Dr. Davison ten thousand dollars then I will give you a loan for thirty thousand dollars over fifteen years."

I was thinking, where would I get another five thousand dollars? "Thank you. That is very generous, and I'd like to discuss it with Dr. Davison. Can I get back to you later in the day?"

Mr. Garner stood up and extended his hand. "That would be fine, Dr. Freed. I'll have some papers drawn up just in case, and I hope to see you later."

"Thank you, sir. I appreciate your time."

I sat in my old Ford truck in the bank parking lot thinking, *how can I do this?* I only have five thousand dollars. I couldn't even afford to rent a house, what was I thinking, planning to buy a veterinary business?

As I drove through the streets on my way back to the veterinary clinic people walking on the sidewalks waved to me. I took Central Valley Road down through the farms, the sun was shining and the fields were green with tall grass. The grass along the road was just turning gold and some fields were being cut, I saw tractors going from field to field. There were deer grazing, and I even spotted a large buck. Flocks of wild turkeys made their way across the fields and the country roads. As I passed some ranch houses, I could see flowers blooming in the neatly cared for yards. What a change from the bumper-to-bumper traffic and the constant noise of the city. It felt good. It occurred to me that I could be a country vet. I drove back to the veterinary clinic.

"Dr. Davison I could give you thirty-five thousand dollars cash for your practice."

Dr. Davison didn't hesitate a second, "*Sold.*"

What had I done? I'd bought a veterinary clinic— my life was about to change forever.

• • • •

Back at work things seemed different. It was still very busy, but now I could see the direction my life was taking. When things got hard or sad I closed my eyes and thought about that beautiful valley that I would soon be moving to. Dr. Irvine, although disappointed with my decision to leave, was quite supportive. He began to lessen my client load as I began making my preparations to move. As word slowly spread, I began receiving going away cards, visits from especially close clients and even some gifts. I was truly touched by these clients that had somehow become much more than that.

I sold or gave away most of my meager possessions so that the remaining items would fit into my pickup to make one trip. My last day was busy, and that night, I finished up my client records, made notes for the other doctors, made a few remaining calls to check on pets, and as the janitorial staff came in I slowly walked through the hospital. I looked into the exam rooms, the pet wards, the surgery room and recovery room, pass the employee lounge and out the back door. The parking lot was empty except for the janitorial van and my pickup truck. The parking lot lights illuminated my truck as I unlocked the door and sat in the cab a while. I started it up, and as I pulled out onto El Camino Real, I looked into my rearview mirror and said goodbye to the Irvine Veterinary Hospital.

Wet, Cold and Jethro

Sunday 3:00 a.m.: Nedders' cow, Jethro, stuck in mud.

There was a lot for me to learn about being a country veterinarian when I bought the Redwood Veterinary Clinic in Willits. Dr. Davison stopped in from time to time to see how I was doing and sometimes I went over to his ranch after work to hang out with him. At the time I thought it would be good to know how to do livestock, small animals, and wildlife so I tried to involve myself in all those aspects. Later, I found it would be best to do a few things well, rather than many things not so well. One day I got a telephone call from Dr. Davison.

"Charlie?"

"Yes."

"This is Bobby. I'm going out of town for a few days, can you cover for me?"

"Sure, Bobby. I can do it."

"Well, I know you haven't been doing any livestock lately. Are you sure?"

"I still remember a few things."

"Cause I could call Dr. Leland. Even though he's retired, he might be willing to help out."

"I can do it."

"But my clients are particular."

"Bobby, it's just a few days. I can do it."

"Well, okay, Charlie. But be extra careful and do your best."

"I will, Bobby. Relax, what could go wrong in a few days?"

• • • •

When the telephone rang, it awoke me from a sound sleep, and I could hear rain on the roof. I turned on the bedside lamp to see that it was three in the morning. I picked up the telephone, it was the answering service, and they had a call for me.

"Is this Bobby?"

"No, this is Dr. Freed. Dr. Davison is out of town, and his calls are being transferred to me."

"Oh, God! I need Bobby!"

"What is it?"

"I need Bobby now!"

"Who is this?"

"This is Fred Nedders, young man, and Bobby has taken care of my Angus herd for the last five years. He knows my cows, and I need him right now. Are you a vet?"

"Yes, this is Dr. Freed. What do you need?"

"Do you know anything about cows?"

Fred Nedders. I can still hear Bobby's words from our last telephone conversation just before he left.

"Oh, Charlie. Fred Nedders, the Angus rancher, his cows will be breeding in a few weeks. I just vaccinated them and checked his prize bull. That bull is amazing. His son, Tommy, raised it from a calf, and it's their pride and joy. It's huge and mean as sin. If you get called out, get him to pay you right then because I always have to bill him three or four times and then he only pays a little bit at a time. Drives me crazy. Oh, yeah, Nancy Richards' sheep started lambing this week. She's been through this a few times, so I don't think she'll call you, but please be careful. She is one of my best clients."

"You there young man?"

"Yes, Mr. Nedders."

"Ain't you the new small animal vet in town?"

"Yes."

"Do you know anything about cows?"

"Mr. Nedders, I'm a graduate of U. C. Davis Veterinary School."

"But this ain't just any cow. This here is Jethro. He's our bull, and without him, my farm ain't worth a plug nickel."

"Well, Mr. Nedders, just what's the problem? Why are you calling me?"

"Well, young man, it's like this—me and Tommy have been trying all night to get Jethro up and moving. He has done got himself stuck in the mud, and we just can't figure out what to do."

This didn't sound like a veterinary emergency to me. "Don't you have any friends who can help you?"

"Well now, that's just it. It's just me and Tommy here this week, and we have no one else to call. It isn't like we haven't tried to get him up, but he's just plumb tuckered out. Every time we try to help him, he just keeps on struggling. I thought maybe you could give him a tranquilizer to relax him and then I could pull him out with my tractor."

That seemed reasonable enough. "Okay, I'll get dressed and be out as soon as I can."

"Can you help us, young man?"

"Well, I'm coming out, and I'll see what I can do. I'm sure it can't be too bad."

"Fine. We'll be looking for you. Remember it's the third road off to the left as you come up the hill."

I put my slicker on and my new rubber boots. I picked up my doctor's case, a lariat that Dr. Davison had left behind, and two coils of rope and headed out to the ranch.

The first gate I came to was suspended over a lake of water. I got out of my truck and swished over to it and as the rain came down, I pulled the gate open through the water. Got back in my truck, drove through, got out of my truck, and closed the gate behind me. I can remember Dr. Dans, from veterinary school, telling us that you always close the gates on a ranch. I was to find out this was the first of four gates to go through. By the time I made it through the fourth gate, I had fallen down twice, gotten water in both my boots, and my slicker was now just a patch of mud. I was getting soaked. I was cold. I was already tired.

Off in the distance, I saw the lights of a barn. A house was set farther away and then I saw two flashlights that were waving me in the direction of a corral. I pointed my truck lights to where they were walking and sure enough, there directly ahead of me was a large black mass stuck in the muck of mud. The bull's eyes shone in my headlights. *He didn't look too tuckered out to me.*

"This here is Jethro, young man, and you can see the trouble he's in."

I hadn't met Fred Nedders, but here he was sitting on his tractor. He looked to be over two hundred pounds, but it wasn't fat. Large muscular arms stuck out from his coveralls. His face was covered in a well-trimmed black beard. He looked down right ominous. His son, Tommy, was the opposite. Thin, blonde, and pale skin, he kept bouncing around from the tractor seat, to the fender, down to the hitch, and back up again. He was in constant motion. And there was Jethro.

He was stuck in a huge mud hole. His right rear leg had disappeared into the mud, and as he struggled, his front feet kept rising and falling into a similar lake of mud.

"Are you going to lasso Jethro, young man?" Mr. Nedders was yelling through the rain. "That's what Bobby would do."

I'd brought the lariat with me, but I'd never really lassoed anything. I wasn't looking forward to making my first attempt in front of these two. "Let me look over the situation first, Mr. Nedders."

Tommy spoke up, "We need Bobby. He always knows what to do."

The rain was pounding down on my head and went down behind my ears, finding its way to my neck. I could feel its cold fingers crisscross down my back and into every crevasse of my body—I was becoming as wet inside my clothes as outside. I walked around trying to think what I was going to do. As I walked through the mud, I felt my feet becoming trapped, and it was difficult to get them out without the danger of losing my boots. But I made it over to the poor animal.

"Pull on his tail, that's what Bobby would do," Tommy offered as he stood atop the tractor. I looked up to see Mr. Nedders' cold stare.

"Bobby would lasso Jethro and then me and him would pull old Jethro out of that mud," Tommy yelled through the rain.

I went back to my truck to get some supplies. I pulled up a syringe of tranquilizer; I got the lariat and the rope. I anchored the end of one rope to the tractor hitch, after Mr. Nedders had pulled it as close as he dared.

"Pop, you're going to get the tractor stuck just like Jethro."

"Mr. Nedders," I yelled, drinking more rain, "bring the tractor a little closer."

"You better lasso him, Doc. Bobby always uses his lariat." Tommy had now moved to the back of the tractor.

I began trying to lasso the bull's head. After about a dozen attempts, much to Tommy's delight, I had it secured and tied to the end of the rope. I had Mr. Nedders pull forward just enough to keep the bull's head from getting me as I slithered into the mud. I gave Jethro the injection.

"That's going to pull too much on Jethro's head, Pop. He'll be too sore to breed."

I looked up to see Mr. Nedders' head shaking back and forth slowly. I took the second rope and pushed and pulled until I got it just behind Jethro's front legs and over his back. This I also tied to the tractor.

"All right," I yelled to Mr. Nedders, "pull the tractor forward until the ropes are taut."

"Pop, you're going to pull his head off!"

"Pull the tractor away slowly, Mr. Nedders. Hold it right there," I yelled to him through the drenching rain.

By this time, my slicker had slithered into the mud, my shirt was torn, my boots had long since disappeared, and I was a walking sponge of mud. As the mud tried to suck me down, I slid and slipped my way around Jethro.

With the ropes pulled tight, Jethro was now in a straight line and couldn't whip his head around; I grabbed his tail and with all my might started to pull him up.

"Go ahead," I yelled, "start up your tractor, but go slow." As the tractor moved away and I yanked up on the bull's tail, Jethro slowly started to emerge from the muck. He was coming out of the mud, and I could see the excitement in Tommy and Mr. Nedders' eyes as they realized I was going to save Jethro. And I would have, if the ropes hadn't started to fray. I watched, horrified, as each one snapped and Jethro slid back into the muddy lake.

"He's going to die in that mud hole, Pop. Isn't he?"

I tried to look calm. The tranquilizer I'd given Jethro was taking affect; he wasn't moving.

"Jethro is just tranquilized, he's okay." I tried to sound confident, but I was desperate as I walked back to my truck and looked over my supplies. Suddenly, I noticed the shine of the chain I used to stretch fences with and the comealong. I pulled them out and started back toward Jethro.

"Pop, that chain will cut Jethro up."

I was starting to wish Tommy would come a little closer to the mud hole.

"Can't use the chain, young man. Can't hurt old Jethro."

I stood there, no slicker, torn shirt, no boots, soaking wet in mud. I took my pants off. I then took the chain and passed it up one pant leg and then down the other. Standing in the pouring rain in my underpants, I put the chain around Jethro's neck, making sure the chain didn't come in contact with his skin. I hooked the chain ends to the comealong and that to the tractor.

"Okay, Mr. Nedders, start the tractor up and pull slowly away." As soon as the chain was taut I yelled, "Stop, hold the tractor right there." I then started to ratchet the comealong very slowly, one click at a time. Jethro slowly rose out of the mud onto solid ground. He looked exhausted and made no attempt to move. I easily removed the chain. I gathered up the broken rope, the chain and comealong, and started to drag them back to my truck.

As I walked out of the corral, I happened to look up and noticed Tommy's mouth was open, but for the first time tonight, he was silent. His eyes were wide open—he was staring back over my right shoulder. I turned my head just in time to see Jethro whip his head around and throw mud everywhere before he looked straight at me and came charging. I don't know where he got the strength or where I got mine, but we both took off running across the fields.

I fell and slid on the ground but the constant grunts and snorts of Jethro just behind me, got me to my feet every time. I headed for the gate. Over I went into the mud, and as I wiped my face, I saw Jethro staring from the other side. I said a little prayer of thanks to Dr. Dans that I'd closed this gate. Jethro threw his head back and forth, stomped the ground, and trotted off along the fence line. I lay there for a while—a sore, filthy, soaking, almost naked, tired mess.

I heard the tractor pull up. "*Doc?*" Mr. Nedders actually sounded worried. "Doc, you okay down there?"

I pulled myself up and smiled at Mr. Nedders. "Yes, Mr. Nedders, I'm just fine, and it looks like Jethro is too."

"I'll say. I haven't seen him move that fast since we brought the heifers in last spring."

•   •   •   •

A few days later Bobby called. How did it go?"

"Fine, Bobby, it all went fine."

"Are you sure?"

"Yes, I'm sure. Why do you ask?"

"Well, I opened my mail, and I have a check for a farm visit to Fred Nedders."

"That's right, I was there. Is there something wrong?"

"No. Nothing, I guess. It's just that this is the first time old Nedders has ever paid me before I've billed him; and he sent seventy dollars extra. Something about a slicker, boots, and a pair of pants?"

Oh yes, the slicker, it had never been found, probably still in four feet of mud with my boots, and the pants, they were ruined.

I smiled. "Bobby, I'll be right over."

The Trip

Tuesday 1:00 p.m.: Consultation with Dr. Niles, coughing cat.

We'd had a busy morning. Terry, one of my technicians, was busily cleaning the surgery packs we had used.

"Terry, I'm going to take these radiographs over to Dr. Niles. I'll be back by 2:30 p.m."

Dr. Niles was a colleague and very good friend. When I'd moved to Willits, Dr. Niles had been the first veterinarian to call me. I remember that conversation.

"Dr. Freed, Ernie is on the telephone for you," Terry called to me that day.

"Ernie who?"

"He just said, 'I'd like to talk to the 'new vet' in town.' But I know its Dr. Niles who owns the Little Lake Animal Hospital south of town."

I picked up the telephone, "Hello?"

"Good morning, Charlie, this is Ernie Niles, and I want to welcome you to Willits."

"Why, thank you, Dr. Niles."

"No, no, Charlie, you call me Ernie, none of that doctor stuff between two colleagues. I want you to know if you ever need any help or to borrow any surgical instruments, you just call me."

"Gosh, Ernie, what a nice thing to do."

"Don't mention it. I'll call you later so we can have lunch together."

Thus was the beginning of a twenty-eight year friendship. He was about fifteen years older than me and had just a wonderful amount of common sense and practical veterinary knowledge. I enjoyed talking with him and getting his ideas on difficult cases.

It also gave me a chance to talk with his wife, Jennifer Niles. She had a great sense of humor. She often would play jokes on me. Many times she had her office staff call with outrageous emergencies. They would always get me going before I realized they were laughing hysterically in their office. Mrs. Niles was a very outspoken woman, a compulsive smoker, but she and Ernie had raised four children, and she kept Ernie's office running smoothly and efficiently.

Today, I had some chest radiographs on a cat I'd hospitalized with difficulty breathing. As I went into the office, Mrs. Niles, who also was his receptionist, bookkeeper, and part-time technician, was talking on the telephone. As I listened, I could tell she was arranging a trip.

"That's Niles. *N-i*-l-*e-s*. Niles. Dr. Ernest and Jennifer Niles. We will be bringing our daughter and her husband, and we want a nice cottage on the lake with a dock and our own boat. My husband likes to fish." There was some silence. "What's that? No. No, that won't do. We want a two-bedroom cottage. Yes, that's right. Good. Let me confirm the dates. We will be coming June 23 and staying until June 28." Again there was a pause. "No. You quoted me $750 plus $20 per day for the boat." Another pause. "That's right. It's set then. We'll be there before four p m on June 23. Thank you. Good-bye."

"Hi, Jenny. Planning a trip?"

"Oh, Charlie, sorry to keep you waiting. I can't wait to get away for a while. You know how much Ernie likes to fish, and I haven't seen my daughter since Christmas. It will be great."

"Where are you going?"

"Tahoe. It's so beautiful there. We were there two years ago, and I saw these really cute cottages right on the lake. I told Ernie if we ever went back, that is where I wanted to stay."

"I'm glad you're getting away. I'll be around and can take any emergencies for you."

"Yes, thank you, Charlie. We really appreciate that." She looked at the folder in my hands. "Are those the X-rays you wanted Ernie to look at?"

"Yes. It's a cat with a breathing problem, but I don't see anything on these radiographs. I hope Ernie can help me."

"Charlie, he's just finishing up a cat spay. Let me tell him you're here." She disappeared down the hall. Pretty soon I heard Ernie's booming voice.

"Come on down, Charlie, I'm almost done!" I passed through the door from the reception room into a hallway that led past his laboratory and pharmacy and down the left to his surgery room. He was just putting the last sutures into the skin when I walked in. He took off his surgical mask and pulled his gloves off. "Hi, Charlie. How are you doing this fine day?" I've never met a person who was always smiling, but that was Ernie. He rarely saw a cloud in the sky, but if he did, *his* clouds always had a silver lining.

I put the radiographs on his viewer and turned it on. The lungs were nice and black. The heart shadow was clear. I didn't see any lesions. Ernie was looking over my shoulder, and when I turned, he had a smile on his face.

"Your kitty is coughing but doesn't spit anything up. The blood tests were normal."

I looked at him in amazement. "Yes."

"This kitty is an indoor cat, and if there are other cats in the house, they have no symptoms of a respiratory problem."

"Yes! Okay, Ernie, what do you see that I don't?"

Ernie stood six foot two to my five foot four so he towered over me. He put his hands on my shoulders. "Charlie, look at those lungs. It's what you don't see."

"I don't get it."

"Well, Charlie, the lungs are perfectly clear. The heart outline is sharp. There is no increased density to the lung fields. Now look at this kitty's diaphragm. Can you see how straight it is? And where are the edges of the lungs? You can't see them because this kitty is sucking in air, but can't get it out. Its bronchioles are closing up because this kitty has asthma."

"Darn it, Ernie! Why didn't I see that? I know about cat asthma, but I've never seen a case."

"Come on, Charlie, let's get some coffee." I followed Ernie down the hall, stopping to fill two coffee cups and then into his office. "But now that you've seen this one, you'll never miss that again."

I was sitting there feeling stupid. "You know, Ernie, it just seems like I have so much to learn. When will I ever know it all?"

"Good God, Charlie! You'll never know it all! That's why they call it *practice*." He laughed. We drank our coffee. I suddenly felt better. Ernie could do that. He had the ability to make me stop and look at the big picture.

"Thank you, Ernie. I'd better get back there and add steroids to the antibiotics it's already on."

"That's right, Charlie. Give it a half-milligram per pound for five days and then try every other day. Plan to treat it for at three weeks gradually reducing the dose. Some of these cases need a low dose every other day for a long time and others you can just treat the occasional bouts."

As I left Ernie, I started to think about the conversation I'd heard concerning their trip. I went to the nearest pay phone and called Mrs. Niles. She answered:

"Hello, this is the Little Lake Animal Hospital. How may I help you?"

I almost started laughing. "Hello, is this Mrs. Niles?"

"Yes, speaking."

"Oh, Mrs. Niles, I'm so glad I caught you. This is Ted Jefferson of Tahoe Holiday Cottages. I believe you are planning to stay with us in June?"

"Yes, we'll be staying from June 23 until June 28."

I cleared my throat. "Yes, that's what I've confirmed.

The problem is I believe you were given the impression that the $750 was for the whole party. I wanted you to know that it's $750 per couple. I hope this isn't going to change your plans?"

"*Change our plans! Change our plans!* Of course it's going to change our plans! You've just doubled the cost of our vacation! How couldn't it change our plans? The lady who took our reservations said it would be $750 for those five days."

"Well Mrs. Niles..."

"You let me finish! I was very clear the dates and number of people that would be staying and the lady said it would cost us $750."

She was livid, and I was afraid I'd gotten over my head. "Well, Mrs. Niles what if we gave you the boat rental for 50% off?"

"So, big deal! You're going to charge us $750 more and give us $50 off for the boat rental? I'm afraid that we'll just have to cancel the whole thing. We can't afford $1500 for five days!"

"I'm extremely sorry, Mrs. Niles. Perhaps I can talk to the general manager, Mr. Freed, and get back to you." A long silence. A very long silence.

"*Charlie is that you?*"

I couldn't hold it any longer and started laughing "I hope you have a nice vacation in Tahoe, Jenny."

"Charlie Freed, you are going to be very sorry. *I am going to get you for this!*"

I was still laughing when I hung up the telephone.

Lightening Fast

Like a fast-flitting meteor, a fast flying cloud, a flash
of lightning.

WILLIAM KNOX

For the first two years after buying the Redwood Veterinary Clinic I lived in the back room at the clinic.
The clinic was a converted mobile home. There was a
refrigerator but the stove had been removed so I got a
hot plate and slept on a cot. The shower worked, so I
got along pretty well. It was during those months that
I realized a cat could actually meow all night long—all
night long, never stopping. I'd get out of bed and walk
back to the kennel room. Silence. I would check the
litter boxes, make sure they were all clean, fill up water
and food dishes, and go back to bed. Within minutes:
"Meow, meow, meow." I never got used to it. It was a
relief once I could afford to rent my own home just
outside of town.

What was funny was for those first two years my clients didn't know I was living at the clinic. They were always surprised at how fast I responded to their emergencies.

"Hello, this is Dr. Freed."

"Dr. Freed! Our dog just got hit by a car! We're on our way!"

I got up, put my clothes on, combed my hair, and turned the lights on, and waited. Soon a car pulled into the parking lot.

"Oh, Dr. Freed, am I glad to see you." I recognize Tom Yardly and his dog, Jack.

"Let's see what you have there, Tom." He put Jack on the exam table where I had a blanket waiting for him. "Well, his pupils are both equal, gums are pink, a few abrasions on this back right leg." I continued my exam of Jack. "Tom, Jack looks pretty good, but just to be sure I want to take some radiographs of his chest and pelvic area."

"Whatever you say, Dr. Freed. I know Jack is in good hands. But, Dr. Freed, there is one thing I'd like to know?"

I was ready for the subject of money to come up next. Always the most difficult part for me. "Yes, Tom?"

"Well, Dr. Freed, I just live around the corner there. How the heck did you beat me to the clinic?"

I smiled. "I always try to be available for my clients, Tom. Why don't you help me get Jack into a kennel until I can get Terry to come back down?"

"Okay, Dr. Freed. Should I wait?"

"No, Tom. This is going to take awhile, and I am going to give Jack some pain medication in a minute so he'll be sleeping most of the night. I think it's best he doesn't move around tonight." We got Jack settled into the kennel. "I'll call you later with the results of the radiographs and then we can make a plan from there."

"I'll be waiting for your call."

I walked Tom to the front door.

"And, Dr. Freed."

"Yes?"

"Thank you for coming down tonight to help Jack."

"No trouble at all, Tom. I'm always glad to help."

I called Terry and she came down to help me with the radiographs. Jack was lucky. No broken bones, and his chest and abdomen looked normal. We gave Jack some intravenous fluids to prevent shock and started him on antibiotics for the bruising that had occurred. After the injection of pain medication, Jack was resting comfortably, and of course, it would be easy for me to keep an eye on him tonight because I was sleeping in the next room. "Thanks for coming down, Terry. I'll see you in the morning."

"No problem, Doc. I've always liked little Jack, and I'm glad he'll be okay. See you tomorrow."

Word soon spread around town about how quickly I responded to emergency calls. I think it was one of the reasons my business grew so much in those early days.

Hazel to the Rescue

Charity begins at home.

SIR THOMAS BROWNE

1980

In 1926 a Frontier Days Committee was formed to raise money to build a hospital in Willits. They decided to hold an annual rodeo, parade, and barbecue with the proceeds to go into a general fund. The Willits' Fourth of July Rodeo is now the longest continuously run rodeo in California.

It was also in 1926 that Charles Howard's son, Frankie, died in a truck accident at their ranch. Mr. Howard had made his fortune as a Buick dealer and owned the Ridgewood Ranch, a seventeen thousand-acre ranch stretching south of Willits to Ukiah. He was the owner of the famous racehorse Seabiscuit. Dr. Raymond Babcock, Willits' physician and surgeon suggested that Mr. Howard build a hospital in Willits to help prevent others from losing a child. Mr. Howard funded the hospital, and completed in 1928, the Frank R. Howard Memorial Hospital still serves the Willits community today. The first Frontier Days profits went to equip the hospital.

One day in June Dr. Davison called me.

"Charlie?"

"Yes."

"What are you doing this Fourth of July?"

"I'm not going anywhere, if that's what you mean."

"Well, you see I've been called out of town that weekend and won't be able to do the vetting this year."

"Yes?"

"So, I was wondering if you could vet the rodeo."

My knowledge of horses and livestock was limited, and I wasn't eager to accept. However, Dr. Davison had given me a good deal on the sale of his practice, and he'd been very supportive the last couple of years.

"Gee, Bobby, you know I don't know much about that."

"There's not much to it, Charlie, maybe a cut or two."

Now that was a relief. "Okay, Bobby, I'll do it."

I'd been to the parade and the barbecue and had watched some of the rodeo last year.

When I walked into the fairgrounds, the arena had been sprinkled with water the night before, but under the July sun, it had turned to dust quickly. The dust clouds circled up to the bleachers covering spectators with a fine powder. Rodeos are intense for the riders, their horses, and the cattle. This time instead of being a spectator, I was part of the "inner circle" so I figured there would be some respect coming my way. I even wore my cowboy boots and my oldest pair of Levi's.

"Hey, Doc, how are you today?" It was Fred Langer, the local accountant and one of the committee members. He stood over six foot, his black hair under his cowboy hat, and with his black bushy mustache, he looked every bit the part of the wild west cowboy. "It sure is a hot one today. Better come over here and stand in the shade."

"Thanks. How is the rodeo going?"

"Just getting started. First the Barrel Racing and

then the calf roping and finally the bull riding. We have a lot of contestants in all the events today."

I could hardly hear the announcer over the roar of the crowd. I looked up to see that the bleachers were full. Spectators were waving their cowboy hats, and some were waving small American Flags. It was easy to get caught up in the excitement.

"Where's Dr. Davison?" Fred was watching the barrel racing.

"He had to leave town, I'm filling in for him."

Fred looked away toward the arena as one horse knocked over a barrel, a five second penalty. "Well, let's hope you won't be needed today."

I wasn't sure if that was a remark about my ability or just wishful thinking.

Fred looked down at me, "Can you do horses, Doc?"

"I think I can handle it."

"Not quite the same as a dog you know, Doc."

Now I was sure what he meant. Don't worry, Fred, I can do it." I felt my confidence slowly eroding so I went in search of a cold drink.

I walked over to the concession stand. Hazel MacKensey was selling beer. She smiled as I approached. I'd met Hazel on two occasions. The first one was when Bobby had me over for dinner. Hazel was his girlfriend, and she cooked a great spaghetti dinner for us. Hazel was about five foot; curly red hair, a cheerful smile, and faint freckles covered her cheeks. I hadn't been able to keep my eyes off her, but she was Bobby's girlfriend and a cowgirl besides. The second time I met Hazel, I'd been on a house call to see a dog with a chronic ear problem. She was giving riding lessons to one of the children at the ranch. As I came out of the house Hazel was just beginning to cool down the horse and brush it out. I walked over to see her, tripped on the hose, and found myself lying at her feet in a puddle of mud. I hoped this meeting would go better.

"Hi, Hazel."

"Hi, Dr. Freed. Would you like a cold beer?"

"Please call me Charlie, Hazel. And I'm vetting the rodeo today, so no beer for me, but I'd take a lemonade if you have one."

She handed me a lemonade with ice. It was just what I needed.

"You're vetting today?"

"Yep, Dr. Davison was called out of town."

She didn't look happy. "Oh yeah, Bobby was called out of town alright. Her name is Elizabeth Welding, and her family has a thoroughbred ranch in Willows. He's been dating her since October. She's a vet student at U. C. Davis."

This was news to me. "You and Bobby aren't together anymore?"

"Not since I walked in on them last November. I went over to his house to get a jacket I'd left there."

It was becoming hotter. I drank some more lemonade. "I'm sorry to hear that. How did Bobby meet Elizabeth?"

"Didn't you know that Bobby is going back to U. C. Davis to become a professor? He's been over there about one week a month now, and I think this September he'll be moving there."

"Gosh, I had no idea. I hadn't heard a word."

Hazel left to help another customer. When she came back I had finished my lemonade. "Anyway, Bobby was teaching a class that Elizabeth was in, and before I knew it, he was suddenly always busy when I tried to get together with him." I handed back my glass. "Do you want another, Charlie?"

"No, I'm going to go back over by the stands and see how things are going. I'm sorry about you and Bobby."

"Don't be. And, Charlie, I'm off at three o'clock."

"I'll be back at three o'clock," I said with a smile. This day was certainly starting to look better.

I got back to the stands. The barrel racing was over and the calf roping had begun. I was standing there talking to Fred when the first two riders came out and went after the calf. They roped the calf and had it on the ground when the calf kicked out, and I could see one of the cowboys go down. He was soon up and the team completed the tie, but as they led their horses off, one cowboy was limping.

"Well, Doc, that one won't need a vet. He's going to need a *real* doctor."

I smiled at Fred, but it was all I could do not to say something.

Veterinarians hear this a lot and soon get used to it. I'd decided long ago not to get upset, but I still felt a twinge when people said we weren't real doctors. I'd spent seven years in college to get my Doctor of Veterinary Medicine degree, and I was a doctor, only my patients have four legs. Sure enough, I soon saw the cowboy over by the ambulance. The next two ropings went fast, and on the third one I saw the horse spin and fall. It wasn't down long, but the noise from the bleachers told me something had happened.

"Doc, this one is for you. Looks like a laceration to the hock."

Oh, why did Bobby have to go off with Elizabeth? I went for my doctor's bag, and Fred led me around to the stalls on the east side of the rodeo stands. We went into one of the stalls, and there in front of me was a horse towering above me, stomping the ground, with blood oozing from its left hock.

"Doc, can you take care of her? She's a darn good roping horse. I trained her myself." It was a young man I'd seen around town, but I didn't know his name.

"Hi, Jeff." A familiar voice came from behind me.

"Hi there, Hazel. Old Rosie here has a cut."

This was more than a cut. Bleeding was steady so I knew a vessel had been injured, and I was looking at one of the suspensory ligaments although I couldn't remember its name.

"Do you need any help, Charlie?" Hazel came over. "I saw you grab your bag, so I took a break."

I looked up into those intense green eyes. "Yes, Hazel, that would be great."

"Charlie, here is the lidocaine to infiltrate the area and skin."

"Thank you, Hazel."

"Charlie, would you like me to get the surgical scrub?"

"Yes, the surgical scrub. I cleaned the area thoroughly but it was still bleeding.

Hazel handed me some betadine soaked sponges.

"Maybe you can use these in the wound until you can find that bleeder and tie it off?"

"Yes, right, Hazel." She then handed me a hemostat, and I clamped the vessel.

Next she handed me the suture material. "I think this 2–0 should work Charlie."

"Yes, right, the 2–0." I ligated the vessel and then sutured the fat tissue over the ligament to protect it from scarring to the skin. Once that was done, I sutured the skin. It looked good. Hazel had laid out bandaging materials for me. I put a support wrap on, finished it with VetWrap.

"Charlie, here's the tetanus antitoxin shot and an injection of penicillin."

"Right, Hazel, thanks for getting them ready. Well, Jeff, that should do it. Be sure to have Dr. Davison check this in two days."

"Will do, Doc, and thanks. You did a good job there."

I cleaned up the used supplies and picked up my doctor's bag.

"Here, Charlie, let me help you." Hazel grabbed my bag. When we got back to my truck and put things away I stood looking at her. She smiled, "What?"

"You knew I didn't know what to do."

"I just thought you could use the extra hands."

"Thank you, Hazel. You made me look good. I was scared stiff."

"Nonsense, Charlie. You did a good job. You can be proud of that."

"Hazel?"

"Yes, Charlie?"

"Could I buy you lunch?"

She laughed that delicious laugh that I remembered from the dinner at Bobby's long ago. "Charlie, you're the rodeo vet. Your lunch is free. But I'd like to have lunch with you."

And we did. We sat on the lawn in the large park next to the rodeo grounds beneath the spreading canopy of oak trees and maples. The rodeo crowds, the announcer, the horses, and cattle were but a distant noise to me as my ears were only hearing Hazel. After lunch, she went back to the refreshment stand, and I went back to the rodeo grounds.

There were more lacerations and chipped hooves to deal with, but I was instilled with confidence and finished the day without any serious problems. I was glad that I had made it through without any mistakes, but I was ready to get back to the small animal work that I was used to.

Rusty's Foot

Wednesday 10:00 *a.m.: Wagner's dog, Rusty, sore on foot.*

It wasn't long before I found the Willits Creamery, a small lunch café that was straight out of the past. It was opened in 1935, and I dare say little had changed. The Creamery was situated on the west side of Main Street in a long, narrow building. When you entered there was only a single counter that went from the large front window down toward the back of the building where it made an angle to the left. At the L shaped counter were fourteen stools, and if you got there at the wrong time, you either skipped lunch there or waited outside until someone left. I tried to get the window seat, but the president of the Bank of Willits almost always occupied this.

Every day, there were three sisters behind the counter: two were twins. All three dressed in identical flowered dresses, white aprons, and matching earrings. The Creamery sisters, as they were called, and their brother were the Clover distributor in town. Each morning one sister and her brother delivered milk to businesses and homes. In the afternoon, she would join her sisters at the Creamery while their brother tended to their farm of Angus cattle.

I'd met their brother and one of their ranch dogs when Dr. Niles had been out of town. Mr. Wagner drove up one morning in an old beat up Chevy pickup.

"Doc, old Rusty here has had a foot infection for over six weeks. Ernie had him on antibiotics; it gets better, but soon as the antibiotics stop it comes back."

I was looking at a McNab, a common ranch dog in Willits. He was friendly and didn't move as I examined his left front leg. Between his third and fourth toes was a draining sore. My first thought was a foxtail wound. Since moving to Willits, I'd seen what these foxtails (pieces of a grass weed that grow all over this area) could do. They could find their way into the ears, nose, inside the eyelids, and between the toes. When they got between the toes they would burrow up the blind tissue web between the toes and penetrate in, causing a draining sore until they were removed.

"Did Dr. Niles check Rusty for a foxtail, Mr. Wagner?"

"Now young man you call me Pete. Mr. Wagner was my dad."

Pete had to be in his seventies. "Okay, Pete." He smiled and I noticed he was missing a few teeth.

"Yes, Ernie kept Rusty one day and he did a surgery on his foot, but couldn't find anything."

Sometimes I'm lucky, such as in this case, because another veterinarian has already done the first steps so I knew not to do that over again. I'd already formed a plan in my mind while listening to Pete and examining Rusty.

"Well Pete, I'd like to keep Rusty for the day and see if I can find out what is going on."

"You're the Doc."

Since coming to Willits I'd heard that more than once. It was a saying that I hadn't become used to, but I was warming to it. These ranchers, who'd seen so many things, were entrusting their working dogs to me. They were giving me their trust. It made me want to try my best to earn it.

At lunchtime, Terry and I anesthetized Rusty. We shaved and scrubbed the area around the draining tract. I then injected into the hole a liquid called Renografin that would show up on x-rays. We radiographed Rusty's leg from his toes to his shoulder. What we found was exciting. The radiographic dye went in a tract from Rusty's toes up his leg between the radius and ulna bones stopping just below the elbow. We surgically prepared that area of Rusty's leg, and when I took him to surgery, I knew exactly where I wanted to explore. As I dissected the tissues, I suddenly had pus draining out. Once this was flushed with a sterile saline solution I could see the remains of a foxtail. I removed the foxtail, saving it to show Pete, and then flushed the surgery site first with saline and then with an antibiotic. After suturing the skin closed, we put a bandage over the incision to keep Rusty from licking it and again he was put on antibiotics.

When Pete came back that afternoon to pick Rusty up I showed him the radiographs, how we had used a dye to find the foxtail and finally the foxtail.

"Well, Ernie was right; it was a foxtail."

"Yes, Dr. Niles was right. The problem was that the foxtail had worked its way further up the leg. I knew I had to try something different because Dr. Niles had already done what any veterinarian would have tried. I'm glad you told me that, so I knew to try this." I could tell Pete was impressed with the radiographs. "I want Rusty to take these pills and have Dr. Niles check the surgery site in seven days."

"Alright, Doc. Old Rusty here appreciates what you've done. When can he go back to work?"

"I would rest him the next ten days, but be sure to discuss that with Dr. Niles when you see him."

• • • •

As I entered the Creamery, the next day for lunch you would've thought I was a movie star. The place became silent as the Creamery sisters told everyone there how I'd found Rusty's foxtail. As their story continued through dissecting of muscle and description of the oozing pus, I noticed most of the customers were putting their sandwiches down as appetites disappeared. However my sandwich was great, and I was able to move to the window seat to finish my cup of coffee.

Oh, Nuts!

Saturday 9:30 a.m.: Richter's dog, Bob, HBC (hit by car).

One Saturday I had an emergency call from a local rancher in town. His working dog had been run over.

I wasn't acquainted with many locals yet, so I didn't know that this particular person was a well-known and respected rancher. He pulled his truck into the parking lot and carried his dog into my clinic wrapped up in his jacket.

Having worked at the San Mateo Emergency Clinic, I'd seen my share of emergencies; not all emergency cases go well. Each time I got called in, I hoped that I'd be able to help the pet and send it home with its owner. On this particular day, I was nervous because when pets are run over there are many potential problems that can involve any part of the body, such as the lungs, abdomen, and bones.

"Hi, I'm Dr. Freed."

The rancher placed his dog on the examine table still wrapped in his jacket.

"Well, Doc, Bob here has a problem down below," he said as he gently pulled the jacket apart.

My fears of abdominal rupture, broken ribs, and legs were soon dismissed. I actually felt the anxiety of worry pass as I looked down on the most unusual injury that I'd seen up to that time. Bob's only obvious injury was that his testicles had ruptured through the scrotal sac. I quickly realized how simple this emergency would be, because all I had to do was neuter Bob and close the two-scrotal tears. But before I could tell Mr. Richter my plan...

Mr. Richter tilted his cowboy hat off his forehead and with a grave look said to me, "Doc, Bob here is the best working dog on my ranch, and I intend to use him for breeding. All my friends can't wait to have a puppy from old Bob here."

I looked closely at Mr. Richter's face waiting for a smirk to appear. It didn't.

"Mr. Richter, as you can see Bob's testicles are laying out on his abdomen and they are covered in dirt."

"Yep."

"But, Mr. Richter, what do you think I can do with this?"

"You're the Doc, I expect you to put them back in."

"Back in!"

"Yep."

"But they're contaminated, and if I put them back in, an infection could go up the spermatic cord into the abdomen. He could end up with peritonitis; at the very least, the testicles will probably abscess inside the scrotal sac. And even if all those things don't happen, I really doubt if he'd successfully breed."

"Oh."

"So surely, Mr. Richter, you can see that the best thing to do here would be to neuter Bob."

"You mean you want to *castrate* my best working dog!"

"Well, yes. I mean it would be the best thing to do. You can see that can't you?"

"Nope."

I was pleading at this point. "But Mr. Richter what else can I do?"

Now Mr. Richter was losing his patience with the new veterinarian.

"I expect you to do your job, Doc. I expect you to put those *nuts* back where they belong."

There was a moment of silence as those words sunk into my brain, and the blood drained from my face. I tried to control my voice and not sound too desperate; I really didn't think I could do such a task. In my short career, I'd only taken testicles out (neutered pets) not put them back in. I didn't know what to do.

"When are you going to do it, Doc?"

"Well...I'm...I mean...I'm going to do it right now, and since I don't have any staff here on Saturday, you'll need to help me."

A broad smile came to Mr. Richter's face. "Well then, Doc, let's get started."

I was so upset and nervous that I didn't even move Bob to the pre-surgery treatment area or into the surgery room. Right there, on the exam room table I anesthetized Bob and began the meticulous job of cleaning the testicles, picking all the little specs of dirt off, washing, and disinfecting the area, over and over again.

"Now, Mr. Richter, I want you to hold Bob's legs just like this and keep an eye on his chest to be sure he is breathing regularly."

I put my head and eyes so close to Bob's privates that all I could see were the scrotal tears, the spermatic duct and vessels attaching the testicles to Bob. I lubricated his testicles with an antibiotic ointment and one by one placed the testicles into the proper scrotal tear being sure that the vessels were not compromised. Then I sutured the inner wall of the scrotal sac separately and then the skin of the scrotal sac. When I was done, I looked up at Mr. Richter. I don't know what I expected; maybe recognition for doing the most miraculous surgery in my career. But when I looked up he just had a solemn expression, like maybe we had just vaccinated some steers.

"Well that's done. I'll be taking Bob home now."

Now I finally lost it, no composure, no professional manner. "Take him home! Bob needs to stay here. I need to continue intravenous fluids and antibiotics and then check his incisions and his temperature in the morning."

"Well fine then. I'll see you in the morning."

"Tomorrow is Sunday, Mr. Richter."

"Yep. What time, Doc?"

I was too tired to argue, "Nine a.m.," was all I could muster.

"See you then, Doc." And with that he was out the door and driving away in his truck.

I moved Bob back to the kennel area and put him

on a big blanket. I put an Elizabethan collar on his neck so he wouldn't injure the surgery sites. I adjusted the intravenous fluids and then went about cleaning up the mess in the exam room that was left after the preparation and surgery.

The next day I sent Bob home with Mr. Richter with instructions on how to care for the incisions and antibiotics for Bob. He didn't come back for the suture removal and I never heard what became of Bob. I was too worried to call and find out if Bob had died, or been destroyed, or taken to another veterinarian to fix what I had done, or any other possible scenarios. I was too scared to call.

Years went by and I never saw Mr. Richter in town or heard anything about Bob from any veterinarian. One year at a Rabies Vaccination clinic (I vaccinated over three hundred pets that day), a dog was lead up to me. I was on my knees and just looking for the spot on the rear leg to put the vaccination in when I heard a familiar voice.

"Don't you recognize him, Doc?"

I looked up to see Mr. Richter holding the end of the pet's leash (actually it was a piece of rope). "Mr. Richter!"

"Yep."

"Is this Bob, Mr. Richter?"

"Yep."

"And he's okay?" I couldn't believe my eyes!

"Take a look for yourself, Doc. And he has sired five litters since we saw you."

Well veterinarians do strange things. When we're out at dinner seminars we often clear the room as our conversations turn to surgery, blood, necropsies, and other gory conversation. So I don't think many people took notice when I crouched down and did an inspection of Bob's privates. And to my relief, satisfaction, and excitement, there were two normal looking testicles!

"Thank you, Mr. Richter. I'm really glad you brought Bob down, and I got to see him."

"Well, he needed a Rabies shot, Doc." And with that Mr. Richter turned, loaded Bob into his truck and drove away.

Tick What?

House call: James' dog, Ginger, can't stand up.

I had worked the morning at the clinic and then went home for lunch. That afternoon I'd arranged to make some house calls. My first one was the James' dog, Ginger, at 1:00 p.m. Ginger was a gentle German Shepherd who couldn't get up. I knew it would be difficult for the James to bring her to the clinic so I had agreed to make a house call that afternoon. It also gave me a chance to drive down into the Ridgewood Ranch.

This property is about fifteen minutes south of Willits and was the ranch formed by Charles Howard, the owner of Seabiscuit. Charles Howard is remembered in our community for his famous horse and our local hospital.

Seabiscuit came to Ridgewood Ranch in 1939 to be rehabilitated after suffering a serious racing injury. He was to go on to win the Santa Anita Handicap in 1940 then retired to Ridgewood Ranch to live out a peaceful life, passing away in 1947. At one time, up to one hundred visitors came a day to visit the famous red horse.

As I drove through the valley, the crisp October air blew through the partially opened window. The sun was shining, and the vineyards were alive with red and yellow leaves. The liquid ambers waved their gold and orange branches skyward. Here and there deer were grazing, and I spotted a few young bucks. Flocks of wild turkeys made their way across the fields.

Driving down the winding road into the Ridgewood Ranch I passed a herd of Fallow deer. These were
descendents of Fallow deer that Mr. Howard bought
from his friend, Randolph Hearst, who had an extensive collection of exotic animals at San Simeon. I always
enjoyed seeing the white deer against the green and
golden hills surrounding Ridgewood Ranch. When
they graze near the highway, there are always brake
lights appearing as people try to figure out what they
are seeing.

I drove into the ranch and past the restored stallion barn that was Seabiscuit's. The weather vane of
a horse and jockey spun slowly on the rooftop. The
James' house was a blue panel modular home with
white shutters sitting with a group of others in a later

development on the property after the Howards sold it. The neat yard and freshly painted fence led me up the pathway to their front door. Before I could knock, the door opened.

"I'm so relieved you could come down," Mrs. James said as she waved me in. "Ginger is in the living room with Harry."

I followed Mrs. James and there lay Ginger at Mr. James' feet. He'd been reading a book, and he put it aside as I entered.

"No need to get up, Mr. James." I knelt down by Ginger. "So what's happened here?"

"Well, Dr. Freed, Ginger seemed just fine yesterday. We went for our usual walk around the ranch like we always do. Then last night I thought Ginger seemed weak in her hind legs, and now, this morning, she can't get up at all."

I was examining Ginger. Her gums were pink, her heart rate normal, no pain on palpation of her abdomen, and her temperature was normal. I tried to remember causes of ascending paralysis: botulism, myasthenia gravis, coonhound paralysis.

"Can Ginger get into any carcasses, dead birds, maybe near a pond?"

"Well, she is always on a leash on our walks, and other times she is in our backyard, but that's all fenced. No, I don't think she could've done that without me seeing."

I continued to look Ginger over trying to rule out various diagnoses. I was getting ready to tell the James that I would need to take Ginger to the clinic when my right hand felt a large, engorged tick just behind her ear. "Tick paralysis."

"What's that, Dr. Freed?"

I showed them the tick I'd just removed from Ginger.

"I think Ginger has tick paralysis. Usually once the tick is removed the pet will get better in 24 to 48 hours."

"You mean one tick can cause her not to walk?"

"Well, it has to be the right species of tick and at the right time and a female tick." I disposed of the tick. "Has Ginger been able to eat and drink this morning?"

"Oh yes, she couldn't get up but when I brought some food and water to her she ate just fine."

I was still debating taking Ginger back to my clinic.

"Here's the plan. If I'm right, Ginger will be much better by tomorrow morning. If she isn't, I'll need to get her to my clinic." I reached into my doctor's bag. "I think I'll take a blood sample from her and run the routine tests just to be sure I don't miss something. Can you help hold her for me?"

"I can, Dr. Freed." Mrs. James knelt down by me. "I'm an old ranch girl. I used to help my Dad with all the calves, sheep, and pigs."

I smiled at her. "This will be a lot easier than that, Mrs. James."

Once the blood was drawn I packed up my case and said my good-byes after petting Ginger. "I'll call you with the blood tests results later this afternoon, and I'll call you again in the morning to check on Ginger."

I drove past the brightly painted stallion barn and up the hill towards Highway 101. I stopped my truck and got out. Standing there, looking down at the ranch, I tried to imagine what it must've been like with the horses, crops, the ranch hands and their families, and all the cars coming in to see Seabiscuit. Now it was quiet and peaceful. The deer were farther up the hill, resting in the warmth of the sun. I took a few pictures and got back in my truck and continued my drive up to the highway. There I turned north going over the hill and down Ridgewood Grade and back into the beautiful Willits Valley.

Ginger's blood tests were normal, and when I called the James the next morning, I was told that Ginger was stronger, still wobbly, but able to walk.

Since moving from the city I'd seen so many things that I'd never encountered before. Tick paralysis, dogs with porcupine quills in their mouths, pets bitten by rattlesnakes, dogs with marijuana toxicity, and pets with gun shot wounds. This was a far different type of practice than the city.

This was country life, there were incredible things to see, and I never knew what the next day would bring. This was veterinary medicine at its most interesting and challenging. I was no longer wearing slacks and shiny black shoes. I wore Levi's, a T-shirt, and old hiking boots, and I was starting to fit into life in Willits.

I felt like I was home.

That's Not Chicken

Friday 9:00 p.m.

It was pouring outside; I was just getting ready for bed when someone started frantically knocking at my door. I went out to the hall and turned the porch light on. It was Hazel; her red curls were flattened to her head.

"Charlie!"

"Hazel, come in out of the rain. Let me get you a towel." I headed down the hall to the bathroom, Hazel was right behind me.

"Charlie, I was on my way home, and I came around that curve on East Road and hit a deer."

I handed her a towel. "Are you okay?"

"Yes, but..." She had the towel wrapped around her head. "But the deer, it's not dead, Charlie. It's crying out and dragging itself around. Can you come out and euthanize it?"

Hazel was crying.

"Sure, Hazel, sure. Do you want another towel?"

"No, this is fine. Can you do it now, Charlie?"

I grabbed my jacket. "Let's drive over to the clinic; I need to pick up some supplies."

The rain was coming down in sheets. We both ran for Hazel's car. "Charlie, can you drive?" She handed me the keys, and we got into her car. I turned on the lights one headlight was out.

"Hazel, one of your lights is out."

"What?" She starred out the windshield. "I hadn't noticed."

"Come on, Hazel; we'll take my car."

We drove over to the clinic, and I filled my doctor's bag with the euthanasia solution and syringes. We then headed down East Road. There were no other cars out in this downpour. I watched the fence posts as the headlights illuminated them. I knew on either side of the road were large, open fields—mostly sheep ranches. Soon there would be lambs jumping and running around the ewes, white and fresh looking, with long dangling tails, the ewes, with their heads down, not taking notice. There were large valley oaks dotting the fields that provided shade in the summer months.

But tonight's rain would make small winter lakes appear, giving the name to the Little Lake Valley.

"Just ahead," Hazel's tired voice said.

I pulled off the road when the headlights caught the frightened eyes of the deer. We got out of the car. I used my flashlight to look it over. It was a doe, and I hoped, for Hazel's sake, we didn't see any fawns. The doe's back legs were useless, but she still struggled to get away. I could see why Hazel was upset, it was very sad.

"Hazel, hold the flashlight for me."

She took the flashlight without saying anything. I pulled up the euthanasia solution; we went over to the doe. I roped her front legs together so she won't cut us with her hooves, and as Hazel held the rope and flashlight, I found its jugular vein and injected the solution. The doe was still.

"Well, Hazel, she's not in pain now. She's not frightened anymore. These things happen, you can't always be prepared when they jump out into the road."

Hazel didn't say a thing.

I untied the rope and put the supplies back in the car. Hazel got in, and we sat there a moment.

"Hazel, I'll get my truck over here in the morning and bury the deer at the clinic. Would you like to help me tomorrow?"

She nodded but again was silent. I drove straight to my house.

"Come in and sit by the fire." I got her wet coat off, and she went to the sofa that was by the wood stove. It was nice and warm. I made some hot tea and gave her a cup. I then went back to my bedroom to dry off and change my shirt. When I returned Hazel was asleep. I took her shoes off, pulled her legs onto the sofa, and put a pillow under her head, then covered her with a blanket.

Since that first moment at Bobby's, I'd thought often about Hazel. Many times I had dreamt of her spending the night with me. But this wasn't how I'd imagined it. I put some more wood on the stove, turned the lights off, and went back to my bedroom. It wasn't long before I was asleep.

The next morning came slowly to me as I became

aware of bacon cooking and the smell of fresh coffee. I put my jeans on and stumbled out to the kitchen. Hazel was standing by the stove. Her back was to me, and I stood there admiring her slender form. She turned around.

"And what are you looking at?"

"Would you believe that I was in awe of your cooking skills?"

She smiled. "No." She handed me a cup of coffee.

"You're right."

"You like your eggs scrambled or sunny side up?"

"Sunny side up."

"Me too."

"Coffee's good."

She got some plates, and when I heard the toast pop up, I went over to butter them.

"You have a good assortment of food and utensils for a bachelor."

"Well, I've had a lot of practice."

"You've never married?"

"No. You?"

"Once."

"Were you married long?"

"Thirteen months. He left."

"I'm surprised."

"That I was married?"

I smiled. "No, that a man would leave you."

She sat down at the table. "I think we were just too young."

"Oh."

We ate in silence. I had a second cup of coffee.

"How did you sleep, Hazel?"

"Soundly. I've forgotten how nice a wood stove is."

"That was some storm last night. When you feel up to it, maybe we should move that doe."

"Of course."

I did the dishes while Hazel took a shower.

"Ready?"

"Yes."

We drove over to the clinic and picked up my truck. We drove back to where the doe had been and got out.

"You sure this is it?"

"Pretty sure."

There was no doe in sight.

"Charlie, it couldn't have..."

"Hazel, I gave her two hundred pounds worth of euthanasia, she didn't move, someone took her."

"Took her?"

"I guess someone saw it and figured they'd get some free venison."

"Oh my God!"

It wasn't a pleasant thought.

"What do you think will happen?"

"I think they're going to have some bad tasting venison." I saw just the hint of a smile come to her lips. "Best not to think about it, Hazel."

"No, best not."

We went back to my house, and I examined Hazel's car, the passenger side headlight was broken, but otherwise the car looked fine.

"Hazel, if you get a headlight, I'll help you change that."

"No need, Charlie. Remember Jeff from the rodeo?"

"Sure I do."

"Well, his brother is a mechanic, and he'll do it for me; we're old friends."

I was already jealous. I told myself to act more mature. "That's good, Hazel, take care."

"Thank you, Charlie."

"Hazel?"

"Yes?"

"The breakfast was really good."

She smiled, and I was mesmerized by it.

"You're welcome."

And I watched her drive out of my driveway and down Valley Road.

No Price on Honesty

Wednesday 2:00 p.m.: Henderson's cat, Tootsie, not eating.

A rural veterinarian sees a wide variety of clients, from the person with a teacup poodle that rarely sees the ground, to the rancher with a working McNab. Veterinarians see clients who just want a Rabies shot to the client who will do just about anything to help their pets live a long and healthy life. This can be a source of wonderful fulfillment for a veterinarian, but other times can cause great sorrow and despair when an owner is not willing to give their pet the care it deserves.

What is even sadder is the client who wants to help their pet but doesn't have the finances to do so. Veterinarians are constantly under pressure to help the pet because "we love animals." Although it's true that veterinarians love pets, the reality is that we are business owners, and the business must succeed if we are to continue to help pets. It's a difficult position to be in.

One summer day an elderly couple came into my clinic. Their cat, Tootsie, was very ill. The husband shuffled into the exam room, struggling with the cat carrier; I reached for it.

"Mr. Henderson, let me take that for you. If you come back to the clinic just leave this in your car, and I'll come out and help you."

Mr. Henderson sat down. "Thank you, it is a little hard to get us both in." He rested as I heard Mrs. Henderson coming down the hall. She was pushing an oxygen tank and the small clear tube climbed up her coat and circled her head coming to lie near her nose. A little hiss noise came as she inhaled. She took the other chair next to her husband. "I'm so worried about Tootsie, Dr. Freed. She is four years old and has always been healthy." She stopped, as her breathing got harder. Mr. Henderson took over.

"My wife has emphysema." He reached over and touched her shoulder. "Tootsie stopped eating a few days ago. She'd been drinking a lot of water, but yesterday she stopped that too. She hardly goes out anymore so I don't know what it could be."

As the conversation went on, I was busily examining Tootsie while my afternoon technician, Lisa, held her. I could tell Tootsie didn't stay indoors all the time because she was obviously pregnant. But she looked sick. Her temperature was 105.

"I take it that Tootsie is not spayed?"

"Oh no, she's not, but she has never had any kittens so we thought she couldn't."

I started giving Tootsie some subcutaneous fluids and gave her an injection of antibiotic. "I think Tootsie needs to stay here, and I want to take some x-rays of her belly."

Mr. Henderson spoke up. "That sounds like a lot of money, Dr. Freed, and we just don't have much. Can't you just give us some antibiotics to take home?"

I put Tootsie back in her carrier to make it easier to talk with the Hendersons. "Well, I could do that, but I just don't think that's the answer. I can feel something in Tootsie's belly, and if she is pregnant, the kittens are probably dead and need to be removed. X-rays could give me some clues."

"Well, you see, Dr. Freed," Mr. Henderson explained, "Neither of us work. We get a little money from the state, but mostly we just get by. I mean, we want to help Tootsie, but we just don't have much savings."

This was the difficult part for veterinarians. We all want to help pets, but we have limits on what we can spend. For some even fifty dollars can be a hardship for the family. And Tootsie's problem could easily run into three hundred or more.

Mr. Henderson signed the euthanasia form and shuffled out of the room. "I'll be in the car, Emma."

Mrs. Henderson was sitting quietly in the chair and tears were appearing and tracing down her cheeks. I handed her some Kleenex.

"Thank you, Dr. Freed." She wiped her face and seemed to be breathing harder. "She is such a comfort to me, Dr. Freed. She will sit with me for hours. She sleeps with me; she's been a good friend." She patted more tears away. "I'm going to miss her."

I tried my best to reassure her and helped her to the car. Mr. Henderson helped her in, and he bowed to kiss her cheek. He thanked me, then he got into the car and they drove away.

I turned and walked slowly up the stairs. Lisa was putting Tootsie into a kennel. "Turn the x-ray processor on Lisa."

Lisa turned to face me. "But they want her put to sleep, Doc."

"Yes. Yes, I know, but let's see what's going on in there."

The radiographs showed two fetuses in the uterus.

"I'm going to change into my scrubs. Get Tootsie ready for surgery."

Lisa didn't say anything and went straight to arranging what we needed. We anesthetized Tootsie and removed the uterus with the dead fetuses. We gave Tootsie more fluids, flushed her abdomen, instilled antibiotics, and closed the incision. We transferred Tootsie to a heated kennel, where she recovered slowly. By the next day, she was meowing for food. Within two days, she was eating and grooming; her temperature was normal.

"Now what, Doc? What are you going to do with her?"

"I'm going to call Mrs. Henderson and tell her I just couldn't put her friend to sleep and hope she doesn't get mad." I picked up the telephone. After three rings, I heard a voice on the line. "Mrs. Henderson?"

"Yes."

"This is Dr. Freed."

"Oh?"

"Mrs. Henderson I've done something that I haven't done before, and I hope you won't be mad. I just couldn't put Tootsie to sleep." Silence. "Mrs. Henderson?"

"Yes."

"Are you all right, Mrs. Henderson?"

"Uh, Dr. Freed, what are you saying? You mean Tootsie is alive?"

"Yes." Silence. "Mrs. Henderson?" Sobbing. "Are you still there? I didn't mean to upset you it's just that I knew she meant a lot to you..."

"Oh, Dr. Freed, thank you, but I don't know how we'll ever pay you."

I'd already decided I won't tell her what it really cost, "Mrs. Henderson the bill is eighty-five dollars, and you can make payments."

"Well, Dr. Freed, I appreciate what you've done, but I know it's more than eighty-five dollars. When can I see Tootsie?"

"I'd like Tootsie to stay here two more days to be sure she recovers and is eating well before she goes home. Why don't you come in on Monday?"

On Monday Mr. and Mrs. Henderson were again in my exam room, and I was showing them Tootsie's incision and sutures. "And I want you to give her this antibiotic twice a day for the next week. Can you do that?"

"Oh yes, Dr. Freed, I can do that; my husband can help me. It's just good to see her again, and she looks so much better."

Mr. Henderson stood up. "Dr. Freed, Emma and I know that Tootsie's care cost more than eighty-five dollars, but your receptionist has already told us that you won't take any more. We gave her fifteen dollars and will pay the rest as soon as possible."

"That's fine, Mr. Henderson, I'm just glad to send Tootsie home with you."

Mrs. Henderson got up and came over to me. I leaned down to hear her. "Dr. Freed, I'll bring some money every two weeks until this bill is paid."

I honestly didn't think I would ever see them again. As I watched them drive away, I told Lisa to wave good-bye since that would be the last we'd see of them.

• • • •

The clinic work continued, and weeks passed, I'd forgotten about the Hendersons until Lisa called to me from the reception desk.

"Dr. Freed. The Hendersons just drove up."

I came out to the lobby just as Mrs. Henderson walked in pushing her oxygen tank.

"Hello, Mrs. Henderson, how is Tootsie doing?"

"Oh, Dr. Freed, you should see her. She is gaining weight, and her coat is so shiny. I don't think she has ever looked better in her life."

"I'm really glad, Mrs. Henderson."

She walked over to the receptionist's desk. "I want to put this toward my bill."

Lisa looked at me, and I nodded. "Thank you, Mrs. Henderson. Let me give you a receipt."

"That's not necessary dear, I know what I owe, and I will be here every two weeks until it's paid off."

And she did. Twice a month she came into my clinic and paid ten dollars. She told me she would pay that bill, and she showed up each time just like she said. Many times I thought that if she ever called me on an emergency I'd be there for her. She loved her Tootsie, she told me up front that she couldn't afford my services, but when all was said and done she kept her part of our bargain. People like that are rare.

The Hendersons had my respect.

Try Your Best

Thursday 4:00 p.m.: McMurty's dog, Sandy, vaccinations.

It was Thursday afternoon when I saw Sandy for her yearly vaccinations. Sandy was a Wolf/Husky cross, tall, with a golden-gray hair coat and a fluffy tail that looped over her back. She was a striking looking dog.

"Doc, can you look at Sandy's left back leg? She seems sensitive when I pet her there?"

I examined Sandy's left side, and when I got to her rear leg, there was a small lump. It was painful to her, and she whined and turned to snap at me as I tried to examine it.

"Dave, I can't examine this well without sedating her. My guess is that it's an abscess. Let's put Sandy on antibiotics and recheck her in two weeks."

"Sounds good, Doc. She's never been away from me so I don't want to leave her here."

On the recheck exam Sandy's lump was smaller, and now it felt like some fluid was inside it. It was still painful to her, but this time she let me examine the area.

"I think this is either a bite or a foxtail wound, Dave. It seems to be getting better but continue antibiotics for another two weeks to be sure."

"That's fine, Doc. You know I don't want to leave her if I don't have to."

"I understand, Dave. We'll just have to see what happens. It's possible this lump might rupture but that will be okay as long as she stays on antibiotics."

Dave didn't bring Sandy back for her recheck appointment, but I knew that he'd picked up more antibiotics. I decided to call him and see what was going on.

"Hi, this is Dr. Freed. Is this Dave?"

"Hi, Doc."

"Dave, how is Sandy doing?"

"Well, something has happened, Doc. The lump is smaller but it won't go away."

"Has it opened?"

"No."

"Look, I know you don't want to leave Sandy at the clinic, but I need to biopsy that area."

"Doc, she's pregnant."

"What?"

"She's going to have puppies. I don't know when this happened because I usually keep a close eye on her, but I remember a few weeks ago she was gone for the day."

"That certainly changes things."

"What should I do Doc?"

"I don't think we have any choice, Dave. Once

Sandy's puppies are weaned let's get Sandy back to the clinic." I was already calculating how long that would be. Probably three more weeks to be born, then six weeks until the puppies were eating on their own. Two months. What would happen to that lump in two months?

• • • •

When I finally saw Sandy I couldn't believe what I was looking at. The lump was now a mass that started just below the pelvic bone, down Sandy's leg and then around to just below her anus. It was the size of a cantaloupe. Sandy was barely using her leg.

"Dave, this thing is so large I don't think I can remove it. What I'd like to do is biopsy it and maybe debulk it, make it smaller, to give us some time to figure out what we can do to help her."

"Doc, I don't want to leave her here overnight."

"Look, Dave, let me bring Sandy in now and you can pick her up this afternoon."

We took Sandy to surgery where I reduced the mass to about half, put some drains in and sent the tissue off for pathology. Sandy went home with an Elizabethan collar on, and I planned to remove the drains in five days.

The biopsy came back a high-grade undifferentiated sarcoma, a cancer. When I saw Dave for the drain removal, we discussed his options that included seeing an oncologist for dogs. At this time, the incision was starting to come apart, and I was afraid it would break open.

"Dave, I think you need to make a decision soon

because I don't think this incision is going to hold much longer. Sandy would probably need an amputation of her leg up to her pelvis followed by radiation treatments." I had consulted with an oncologist when the pathology report came back.

"You mean Sandy would lose her leg?"

"This mass seems attached to the bone of her pelvis, and that's the only way to completely remove this type of tumor." Dave was shaking his head.

"No, Doc, I can't do that to Sandy."

"Then I need to clean up this area and try to suture it better." This was an afternoon appointment, and I won't be able to start the procedure until after five o'clock. "Sandy would have to stay overnight."

"Doc, you know how I feel about that, but I can see she needs help. Can I pick her up in the morning?"

"Sure, Dave, but I want you to realize the mass will still be there I'm only going to try to suture the incision better. She'll need to wear that collar again."

"Whatever you think needs to be done, I'll do it. I just can't have her leg amputated."

I discussed with Lisa what my plan for Sandy was.

"How long do you think this will take, Doc?"

"If we get started by six o'clock I should have you home by seven thirty."

"That's good, Doc. I'll get the surgery room ready between our appointments."

We got started at five forty-five that night. With Sandy unconscious, I looked over the surgery area and again palpated the mass. Once she was prepared for surgery, I draped the area off and started to clean up the incision.

"Doc, what are you doing?"

"I think I'll try to debulk this mass some more, so I'll have some loose skin to close the wound better." I began blunt dissecting and soon found I could peel the mass from under the skin. I found that I could work my way around the sides and finally up to the attachment at the pelvic bone. This I surgically cut through.

"Doc, its eight o'clock."

"Oh Lisa, I'm sorry I didn't expect to do this much."

"Don't worry, Doc, it was great to see how you did that. You really got it off. I can't believe it."

"Sandy should feel better with this gone, but I doubt that my surgery edges are clear of tumor. It will probably grow back at some point, but hopefully we can give her some more time."

• • • •

Eight days later, we saw Sandy to remove the drains and check the surgery site.

"Look Doc, she's walking on her leg." Lisa was smiling, and we were watching Sandy walk around the exam room.

Sandy was walking normally, the incision looked fine. There was one draining area at the top of the incision, but I felt that would heal on its own. I'd scheduled Sandy for six injections of an immunostimulant that I injected around the surgery site but mostly up by her pelvic area every week. By the time Sandy came in for her sixth injection, the incision was healed, and she was walking normally. During this time, we also saw her puppies in for their vaccinations.

"Doc, thank you so much. Sandy is doing great, and you should see her with her puppies! She's teaching them all of her good traits." Of the three puppies, one looked just like Sandy.

. . . .

Eleven months later I saw Dave with the puppies for their yearly exams—without Sandy.

"Dave, I'm almost afraid to ask you about Sandy."

"Doc, Sandy passed away last month. She started to cough badly (the cancer had spread to her lungs) and then one night she passed away in her sleep."

"Gee, Dave, I'm sorry to hear that."

"Oh no, Doc! Don't be. You made Sandy pain free for the remainder of her life. She was running and playing with her puppies. I wish you could've seen her. I got to watch her teach her puppies; she was great with them. So, Doc, don't be sorry."

"Well, thank you for letting me try. That day I did the last surgery I was only planning to clean the area up. I never expected to actually try to remove that large mass, but now I'm glad I did."

"Thank you, Doc, you gave me and Sandy ten valuable months together. Thank you for that."

Some clients become like family. Dave was one of these. We hugged each other, and I started to feel tears but held them back. Dave stepped back and looked at me. I couldn't talk. He smiled and shook his head.

"I know, Doc, I know. That's one of the reasons I come here. You really care."

From my exam room window, I watched Dave as he loaded the puppies into his truck. It isn't often, but this time I knew I'd made a difference. I wiped my eyes and picked up the next client file.

Merry Christmas

Monday 3:30 a.m.: Kindell's dog, Tess, dystocia.

The rain was pounding and the wind howling all that night of December 24, 1989, so when the telephone rang, it was one of the few times an after-hours call didn't disturb my sleep; I was already lying awake. I reached over to pick up the telephone and saw the time was 3:30 a.m. *Merry Christmas.*

The frantic voice on the other end was gasping between words, "Doc, Doc, Tess is in serious trouble; you have to see her right now." Even with the panic in his voice, I could recognize Richard Kindell.

Tess was a miniature dachshund and was seven years old now. I'd seen Richard in my veterinary clinic a few weeks before.

"I know you told me that it was time to retire Tess, Doc, but I just had to have one more litter. I've always found good homes for her puppies, but I've never kept one for myself. I wanted to have one of her puppies."

That day in the office, Richard was very apologetic,

and I had to admit Tess was just the best little mother with the sweetest disposition. I couldn't really blame Richard. "Well, Richard, let's see what you and Tess have going on." We took Tess down to the radiology room and took two radiographs of Tess' enlarging belly. One view was on her side and one was on her back, and I counted four puppies to be coming soon. Richard was delighted. We went back to the exam room, and I finished my examination of Tess. Her vaccinations were current, she was taking her heartworm prevention and her last blood tests were normal. "It looks like you'll have four puppies to choose from, Richard."

"Thanks, Doc! I'll see you after they're born for an examination of Tess and her family."

And that was the last I'd heard from Richard until his call tonight.

"Richard, try to calm down and tell me what's happening," I said in a tired voice.

Richard was talking fast, "She had her first puppy about a half hour ago, and she isn't taking care of the little thing. She's lying on her side, straining, and she keeps looking up at me. I know something is wrong; I just know it. Why did I breed her again? I should've listened to you. I don't want to lose her." He was pleading now.

"Richard gather up Tess and her puppy and meet me at the clinic; keep them warm, and I'll see you in a little while." I hung up the telephone and as if on automatic pilot, got dressed and drove down to the clinic. On my way I passed the brightly lit houses with the Santas and deer, the icicles, and the many Christmas lights. The houses were dark inside, but I knew shortly the children would be waking their parents with all the excitement that only this day can bring. My car was freezing inside, but at that moment, it just didn't seem to matter; I was numb from lack of sleep.

I pulled up to the veterinary clinic just as Richard's car was coming into the driveway. I ran inside and turned the outside lights on and got the exam room ready.

"Thank you for coming in; you just have to help poor Tess." Richard had Tess and her puppy wrapped in a blanket. We placed them on the exam table and I looked at the puppy first. "You have a little boy here Richard, and he looks good; keep him warm as I look Tess over." Tess was indeed straining and I tried to exam her vaginal tract with a sterile, lubricated gloved finger but couldn't feel any puppy. "Let's go down to the radiology room. We need to find out what is causing this problem." Again I took two radiographs and I could see the next puppy coming into the birth canal, but with its hind end coming out first. It appeared the back legs were caught on the brim of the pelvic inlet.

"Richard I think Tess will need surgery; Caesarian surgery to save her puppies."

Richard's face turned pale, and he nuzzled the first puppy up to his cheek. "Why did I do this? Tess is going to be all right, isn't she? She isn't going to die? Tell me, Doc, Tess isn't going to die?"

I put my hand on Richard's shoulder. "Richard, you know we can't leave Tess like this, so she has to have surgery. Let me call one of my technicians in, and we'll do our best for Tess and her puppies."

Richard looked down at Tess and then back to me.

"Doc, I know how this sounds, but Tess is the one. I want the other puppies, but it's Tess that has to live tonight. You know what I mean?"

"I know what you mean, but let's not think like that right now. Let's see what we can do."

Soon Terry was at the clinic. "Merry Christmas, Charlie. I think this is the first Christmas I've been up before my kids. I told my husband he'll have to control the troops until I get back. What's up with Tess?"

"Thanks for coming in. Tess has one puppy backwards, and I'm afraid to give her any oxytocin (a drug that causes the uterus to contract and sometimes helps deliver puppies) because I think that puppy's hind legs won't pass through the pelvis." I showed Terry the radiographs, and she went about preparing the prep table and anesthetic machine. I went back to the exam room where Richard and Tess were waiting. I had set up a controlled heating pad with a blanket for the puppy, and it was resting for now, but I knew it would need to nurse soon.

"Richard, I'm going to take Tess now, and I'll let you know as soon as I can what happens." Richard reluctantly put Tess into my arms, and I went back to the prep room. We put Tess on a towel that covered the prep table, and using an anesthetic by mask, we anesthetized Tess. When Tess was unconscious, we intubated her and connected the endotracheal tube to the anesthetic machine and respiratory monitor. We got the instruments ready and shaved her abdomen to prepare her for surgery. "Wait a minute, Terry; let me examine Tess now that she is more relaxed." Terry held Tess on her side and once again with a sterile, lubricated glove I tried to feel the puppy with my index finger. This time I could feel a tail. "Terry, I want you to place your hand right here on Tess' belly and just lightly apply some pressure." When Terry did this I could now feel the puppy's tail and little hind end and just make out the hips. I told Terry to relax a little, and I then pushed the puppy back inside. This time when Terry put some light pressure on Tess' belly, I had my finger ready on the pelvic brim, and as the puppy came up and over, I hooked my finger around its right rear leg. Soon I had wiggled the puppy around until both back legs were over the brim of the pelvis and coming down the canal. I looked up at Terry.

"I know that look, Charlie." She smiled at me. "You've got the little guy, haven't you?"

And just then I pulled the puppy out. "Terry, get some oxytocin ready and disconnect the anesthetic." While I gave the oxytocin to Tess, Terry was cleaning the puppy and using a hand aspirator to clear the puppy's mouth.

"I don't think it's going to make it, Charlie." Terry looked up at me.

"Look, take Tess up to the kennel room, get her on a heating unit, cover her with a blanket, and pull the endotracheal tube when she is ready. I'll be right up."

I grabbed the epinephrine and dopram to try to stimulate the puppy's heart and lungs. A few drops of each on its tongue and then I began CPR. I put my mouth over the puppy's mouth and gently breathed into it as I watched its chest expand. I did this for about five minutes repeating the drugs and CPR, but I had to admit that it just wasn't to be.

At that moment, Terry called to me from the kennel room, "Charlie we have another puppy and Tess is cleaning it and it's already starting to nurse." I ran up to the kennel room, and sure enough, Tess was being the good mother that she had been many times before.

I went back to the exam room and told Richard what had happened. "But the good news is that I didn't have to take Tess to surgery, and she has another puppy that is doing well. Let's take this puppy back and get it nursing."

"Boy, I'm glad Tess didn't have to have surgery."

We put the first puppy with Tess and soon she was nuzzling it over toward the third puppy and before too long the two puppies were nursing side by side. I turned to look at Richard, "I know this is going to sound strange to you Richard, but I feel Tess needs to know what happened to the puppy that was stuck." I could tell by Richard's eyes that he didn't agree with me, but I went down to the prep room and gathered up the little puppy and brought it up to the kennel where Tess was. I placed the puppy down by Tess' nose. She sniffed it and licked it, and before I knew she had picked it up and was growling at me.

"Doc! What is she doing? I've never seen her act like this."

This wasn't what I had expected, and I tried not to look too alarmed in front of Richard. "Tell you what Richard, let's close the kennel door and leave Tess alone for a while. She still has one more puppy inside and maybe we should just let her rest for a minute before we do anything more."

I took Richard back to the exam room, and Terry

went back to the prep room to begin cleaning up. I turned the kennel room lights off and set my hand timer for ten minutes.

"Charlie, what if she bites the puppy or..."

"Don't say it, Terry, I just can't think about it. But don't let Richard back there until I check everything out." I started helping Terry, and before my timer went off, we heard the sounds of puppies nursing and suckling and the general motions of a mother caring for her pups. "I can't wait any longer, Terry; I'm going up to take a peek." Using my penlight I looked in at Tess, and there were four puppies nursing all side by side with Tess holding them near her belly with her head and neck stretched around the group. Four? I looked again. I went over and turned the lights on and went back to look. I counted again. By that time Terry was behind me looking over my shoulder, and we said in unison, "Four?"

"I can't believe it, Charlie! I was sure that puppy was dead!"

I was too busy staring at them and my heart was racing.

"Richard! Richard, come back here; you have four little puppies!"

He looked into the kennel and opened the door. Tess licked his face and he petted her head and each puppy. "Doc, I just knew you could do it." It was all he said, and Terry and I walked back to the prep room.

"Charlie, what did you do? That puppy was gone."

I just stood there waiting for my heart to slow down. "You know, Terry, I can't explain it. I'd given up on it, I expected Tess to push it aside when I took it to her and then I was just going to take it away. I just thought she should know what happened to her little puppy." Shaking my head, "I guess Tess knew differently."

Within the hour Richard was in his car with Tess and her three boys and one little girl, all warm and sleeping. "Thanks, Doc. Thanks, Terry. I'll see you Wednesday and pay my bill. Thank you so much." He pulled his car out and drove away.

"Terry, its six thirty on Christmas morning go home to your family."

"But I was going to finish cleaning up and help you with the morning treatments as long as I'm here."

"Don't worry about that, Terry, I'll treat these other patients and finish cleaning up. Go home and open presents."

"Merry Christmas, Charlie." She smiled and went to her car.

"You too," I shouted to her and closed the door, locked it, and went back in to write up my records, log the drugs that I'd used, and start the morning of treating the hospitalized patients and cleaning the kennels, walking the dogs—the usual things that all veterinary clinics do every day of the week, weekends, holidays, every day. The hours seemed to just pass by, and at some point, I was aware of a knocking on the front door. I pulled my head out of a kennel that I was lining with newspapers, got up, and went down the hall. There was Richard standing at the door. All I could think was the worse. A puppy had died; Tess was bleeding. I opened the door.

"Richard?"

"Don't worry, Doc, Tess is sleeping, the puppies are

sleeping. My sister came over to watch them for awhile for me." As he said this he placed a warm pie in my hands. "I know you like apple pies, Doc, so while I was keeping tabs on Tess and the pups, I made you one." He then bent down and gave me a big bear hug. "Merry Christmas." He got in his car and drove away.

It was a Merry Christmas.

Christmas Dinner

Monday 8:30 *a.m.*

I was still at the clinic writing up Richard's record when a familiar car drove into the driveway. I walked to the front door just as Hazel walked up.

"Hazel?"

"Hi, Charlie."

"Come in out of the cold. How are you?"

She took her wool cap off and shook her red curls loose. "Terry called me, said you're all alone on Christmas."

"I just sent some puppies home."

"Yes, Terry told me." she looked around. "Do I smell apple pie?"

"Yes."

"I guess you have other admirers."

"What? Oh, no. Richard Kindell baked that for me. It was his puppies."

"What are you doing after this?"

"Nothing."

"Charlie, why don't you come with me? I'm headed over to my folks for Christmas dinner and you can bring that pie."

"Hazel that would be wonderful."

I followed Hazel's car down through the valley. I'd decided it would be best to take my car in case I got another emergency. Hazel turned down a dirt road. The rain had left puddles and a few holes were deep so I drove slowly. On my right, I passed a large red barn, the paint peeling on the west side and one door hanging by only a hinge; it was tilted and looked ready to fall. The wooden corrals weren't in any better shape; here and there boards were missing, others broken. It seemed a shame that it was in such disrepair. On my left were open pastures, but I didn't see any livestock or horses.

I followed Hazel up to a carport where a Ford pickup and a Taurus station wagon were parked. I got out of my car.

"I use to ride a lot when I was younger. I was even runner up for the Frontier Days Sweetheart one year," Hazel said as she led me up to the front door. I noticed a handicap walkway had been added. Hazel tapped on the door lightly and walked in, with me following right behind.

The entry way was dark, and the large red tiles looked worn from years of use. We went down a hall that led to a large open kitchen at the other end of the house. There, a window gave a wonderful view of a pond with willows around it. Mrs. MacKensey was doing dishes, and as we came in, she turned, grabbing a towel to dry her hands. She was very young looking, brown hair with just the beginning of gray and a smile that reminded me of Hazel's and very intense blue eyes.

"Hi, Mom. Do you need any help?"

"Oh, Hazel, there's lots to do, but we have plenty of time." She looked at me, "And you must be Charlie."

"Hello, Mrs. MacKensey."

"Hazel has been telling me all about you, Charlie."

"Mom."

"I'm glad you can spend Christmas with us. It's nice to see Hazel happy again."

"Mom!"

"Why don't you show Charlie around, Hazel. Your dad is in the den."

"Come on, Charlie."

So Hazel was telling her mom about me. I watched Hazel walk down the hall with her red curls moving slowly against the back of her neck. She was just a shade taller than me. I guess I hadn't noticed before. Her jeans fit her really well, and I felt Mrs. MacKensey was watching me. I guess there was no secret; Hazel was definitely occupying my mind more and more. I followed her into a bedroom. It had to be hers. The first thing I noticed was all the trophies and blue ribbons, and there were many pictures of a young Hazel riding a horse.

"Very impressive, Hazel."

She spun around. "Come here, Charlie."

I walked over, and she put her arms around my neck. My arms circled her waist, and she moved closer. She felt right. Looking into her eyes made me feel warm. And we kissed for the first time.

"Close your eyes, Charlie."

I did. We stood like that a long time.

"I like you, Charlie."

"That's good."

"Well?"

"I'm afraid to say anything, Hazel, because I might wake up and find this is just a really good dream."

"Come on, silly, I want you to meet my dad."

Down the hall was a den with a stone fireplace and a fire going giving warmth to the room. Split oak and madrone wood was neatly stacked on the side. The walls were knotty pine, reminding me of a house I once lived in. A television was on, but the sound muted. A sturdy man was sitting in a chair next to the fire, and alongside him was an empty wheelchair. As Hazel and I walked in, he put his magazine down and turned to face us. His hair was graying, but there was no mistaking its red color or his red mustache. I looked again at Hazel's curls.

"Dad, this is Charlie."

"Nice to meet you, Charlie. I'm Dan."

I walked over and put my hand out. His grip was strong, with a calloused hand, "Nice to meet you Mr. Mac—"

"Dan, Charlie. You call me Dan." He let my hand go.

"Nice to meet you, Dan."

"Sit down. Sit down. Hazel, get Charlie something to drink."

"Charlie?"

"Pepsi?"

"I'll bring you something." She smiled, kissed me on my cheek, before she walked down the hall.

I looked over at Mr. MacKensey. He blinked at me. He stared at Hazel as she walked out.

"Charlie, she's something."

"Yes, sir."

"Dan."

"Yes, Dan. She is."

"Just between you and me, I'm glad Bobby is out of the picture."

"Oh?"

"He wasn't the one."

"Oh."

"I've heard a lot about you from my neighbors. Sounds like you've really built that practice up. You're getting a good reputation."

"Thank you."

"We don't have any pets or livestock anymore." He looked down at his legs. "Two years ago I fell off the barn roof while doing repairs."

I didn't know what to say.

"Takes a lot of getting use to. I'm not as mad as I use to be."

I shook my head.

"Anyway, it's Christmas. My daughter is happy. That makes my wife and me very happy."

"Yes."

"It's you, Charlie."

"What?"

"She talks about you all the time."

Just then Hazel came in with some hot apple cider.

She looked at her father and then me as she handed me the cider.

"I should've known not to leave you two alone." She turned to her father. "Please tell me you haven't embarrassed me."

Mr. MacKensey winked at me. I winked back.

"I don't want to know." Hazel turned and went back down the hall.

"Use to be a bronc rider," he said and pointed to the wall behind me. "Member of the Rodeo Cowboy Association. Used to travel doing all the rodeos across the U. S. Rode twice at Madison Square Gardens in the National Rodeo, won once."

I got up and walked over to the wall. It was covered with pictures of a young man on horseback. Trophies were displayed, silver buckles sparkled, and there were spurs and horseshoes all in a walnut display case.

"Made enough to buy this ranch and build this house. Those were great times."

"I'm sorry about your accident."

He looked over at the wheelchair. "It's not easy, but you go on. You have to."

"You must've seen a lot of country during your rodeo days."

He smiled and looked again over at the wall. "Incredible country, Charlie. I made a lot of friends over those years. Many of them have been out to visit me. Really picks up my spirits, I can tell you."

"Thanks for including me in your Christmas." I walked back and sat down on the sofa across from him.

"Hazel's had some rough times, Charlie. She was married once."

"She told me."

"Did she tell you he used to hit her?"

"No."

"That was before my accident. Last time I saw him I told him I'd beat him to death if he ever hit her again. Next day he was gone."

"I didn't know."

"And Bobby, nice guy, don't get me wrong, but he'll never marry. Just likes to play around."

I decided not to think about that.

"Well, Hazel was pretty down, just going through the motions, and then about five months ago, we noticed she was acting more like her old self. Right around the fourth of July." He laughed. "Hazel told us about the time you fell into a puddle of mud."

I smiled and nodded.

"Anyways, it's good to see her happy again."

"Dinner is served." Mrs. MacKensey had come in. "Dad, you ready?" She came over and kissed him.

With his muscular arms Mr. MacKensey easily transferred himself from his chair to the wheelchair. As he wheeled himself down the hall, Mrs. MacKensey rested her hand on the back of his neck. I followed at a distance thinking of the affection that simple gesture implied.

The dinner was great, and the whole time I sat across the table from Hazel. Life was definitely good.

Seventeen Cats

House call: Towers' cats, vaccinate at home.
I answered the telephone.

"Dr. Freed?"

"Yes, this is Dr. Freed. How may I help you?"

"Well, Dr. Freed, this is Elizabeth Towers."

The name meant a lot. Mr. and Mrs. Towers couldn't say no to any cat. At last count they had seventeen *indoor* cats. The Towers were very nice clients and quite well known in town. Mrs. Towers, in her early seventies, was an avid reader, forming a local woman's book club. She was also a published author of poems, donated many hours with the Friends of the Willits Library, and taught English to adults in the Literacy Group. Mr. Towers had been a successful photographer in New York City, and even in his seventies, he could still be seen taking pictures around town.

"Yes, Mrs. Towers?"

"Well, Dr. Freed, my husband hasn't been well, and

he usually helps me get our kitties in for their yearly exams."

Each year they would bring four or five cats at a time to the clinic and gradually over the year, get all seventeen in for their examinations and vaccinations.

Mrs. Towers continued, "I was wondering if you could make a house call this year to check our kitty family. I could pay you extra for your time."

"Well, Mrs. Towers, perhaps I could do it one evening after work. Would you be able to confine them to a room to make it easier?"

There was hesitation on the telephone, I could hear her talking with her husband; soon she was back. "Of course, Dr. Freed. We could have them all rounded up, and my husband has all their vaccination histories on his computer. He can print out a copy and we can use that."

I had all their pets' information in my records, but there was no reason to point that out. "That sounds like a good idea. These computers are really becoming something."

"Oh my, yes. My husband does everything on his computer now. He's on it all day long."

"I'll plan to come over Thursday night."

"Thank you, Dr. Freed. We'll be ready. What time should we expect you?"

"Well, my last appointment is five thirty, I think I could be there around six thirty."

"That's just fine, Dr. Freed. Thank you so much."

"It's quite alright, Mrs. Towers."

So it was arranged that Thursday night I'd make a visit to the local "cat house."

• • • •

I walked up the stairs that tilted slightly to the south, carrying my doctor's case that, among other items, had pre-drawn vaccinations for rabies, feline leukemia, and feline distemper. I had to smile at the brass woodpecker doorknocker. I could hear a commotion inside, so I knocked louder. Soon a shadow appeared behind the curtain covering the front door window. The door opened one inch.

"Is that you, Dr. Freed?"

"Yes. Good Evening, Mrs. Towers."

The door quickly shut. More noise and voices of various cats' names could be heard. The door opened one inch again.

"Dr. Freed, you must come in quickly so the kitties don't get out. One. Two. Three!"

I slid into their house as the door quickly shut behind me. There were cats everywhere. Cats on the floor. Cats on the bookshelves. Cats on the stairs, on the table, on the countertops. Cats under chairs and on top of the sofa.

"Mrs. Towers, I thought you were going to confine the kitties to one room."

"Oh Goodness Mercy, Dr. Freed. That just won't do. Susie gets mad at Freddie and Miss Priss only likes our kitchen. Why that just won't do at all."

My eyes followed over all the cats. This was going to be a very long house call. Mr. Towers approached me.

"Dr. Freed, here's a list of all the kitties and a place

for you to check off the vaccinations you give and when they are due next."

He was proud of this, and I had to admit, for a man in his late seventies, jumping into computers was an accomplishment.

"Thank you, Mr. Towers, this will be very helpful. Let's see, the first one on the list is Sesame." I took the syringes from my case. "Now, which one is Sesame?"

"She's the orange tabby that just went behind the stove." Mrs. Towers was smiling. "Here, Sesame. Here, Sesame. Good girl." Mrs. Towers was on her hands and knees, but soon Sesame was in her arms. I gave Sesame her vaccinations and away Sesame flew up the stairs, and she was gone. I checked Sesame off the list, only sixteen more to go.

War and Pain

There is many a boy here today who looks on war as
all glory, but boys, it is all hell.

-GENERAL SHERMAN

Mr. Ruters stared across the exam table. He was a good
six feet, but now with age, was stooped. His San Francisco Giants cap covered what little hair was left. He
was a World War II veteran. Over the years he had told
me about his war experiences. None were good. As he
had told me:

"I had to wipe the bone, flesh, and blood of the
second gunner from my eyes to see to fire. It was the
morning of December 9, 1944, in Marseilles, France.
When the ammunition ran out we fought with the bay-
onets on our rifles. One by one we were captured, and
I spent the next four months in POW camp. The beat-
ings, little food, being hung from fences by our wrists
against the barbed wire, it took its toll."

In spite of this, when back on American soil, he worked for thirty-two years, raising a son and daughter.

Now Mr. Ruters looked down at the exam table at Badger. Badger was a thirteen-year-old Australian Shepherd. His back legs had finally gone out on him, and I was getting ready to administer the euthanasia solution. As I shaved Badger's leg and put the catheter in, I thought about all that this man had been through. The atrocities he had witnessed and yet this strong man was readily allowing his tears to flow as he said his last good-byes to his faithful friend, Badger.

"I am starting the injection now, Mr. Ruters."

He nodded but didn't look up, his attention only to Badger. His head was close to Badger's ear. "You've been a good chap, old Badger. We've been on many an adventure." Mr. Ruters wiped his eyes with his handkerchief. Badger slipped into unconsciousness. "Is he gone, Doc?"

"Badger is out of pain now, Mr. Ruters."

"Yes. I know pain, young man, and I didn't want old Badger to suffer that way."

"I'm going to step out of the room Mr. Ruters and give you some privacy." I walked out and slowly closed the exam room door. Yes, I'm sure Mr. Ruters knew first hand about pain.

Love is Universal

House call: Larsen's dog, Groucho, euthanasia.

In the city, I was used to clients who did the utmost for their pets. I was used to pets freshly bathed, and I was used to some pets that looked as if they never touched paw to ground. I didn't realize that clients could be any different, so my first weeks in Willits had been a crash course in cultures, attitudes, and businesses. I saw ranch dogs, junk yard dogs, I saw occasional pampered pets, and, in the 70's and 80's, I saw a lot of, shall we say, alternative agricultural dogs. Dogs that had that aroma of a certain substance that can be used "for its medicinal properties." I once saw a dog that had been cut on its back; apparently it had been too close to the "harvester." On most of these cases, I was offered payment in a plant substance instead of check or credit card. When I'd decline, I'd always be paid in cash.

At first, I was surprised at how open these people were with me, but as the years went by, I became accustomed to the fact that not all my clients were ranchers, teachers, or employees of banks or hardware stores.

It was one of these clients, Pete Larsen that I came to admire because of his attachment to his friend Groucho. Groucho was part Pit Bull and part Sharpei, and as the years passed, I became quite fond of him. I watched him grow from playful puppy, to mature adult, and then into his declining years. It was sad, but each time I saw Groucho—even toward the end of his life—he still had that happy sparkle in his eyes and that funny curled tail was always wagging.

The day came that Pete asked me about euthanasia. "Do you ever do house calls, Doc?"

I didn't hesitate; I said that I would. All euthanasias are a sad time for me, and even though I can rationalize that it is the humane thing to do, I still find myself saddened, sometimes crying and other times just sitting in my office at the end of the day with flashes of memories passing by.

A few weeks later Pete stopped by the clinic.

"Doc, Groucho has stopped eating. Doc?"

We were standing outside my clinic under the awning, out of the sun. I could smell the sweet fragrance of the narcissus out by the sidewalk.

"Yes, Pete." The last time I'd seen Groucho was about two months ago. He was fourteen now. *How could fourteen years pass so quickly?* He seemed happy, but he'd lost six pounds, he had no conscious control of his right hind leg causing it to frequently trip him as he walked. It was sad to see.

"Doc? Groucho stopped eating two days ago."

I looked up at Pete. He was five foot eight, about

148 pounds with red hair. He wore jeans and a tie-dye T-shirt; a gold earring hung from his left ear. The sun would catch the earring and shine in my eyes from time to time as we stood there.

"Yes, Pete. I heard you. What do you want to do?"

Pete looked up. "I want him to be happy, run again, and live forever. That's what I want, Doc." Tears were forming in the corners of his eyes; he used his T-shirt to wipe his face. I put my hand on his left arm, and he put his right hand over mine and gave it a quick squeeze then turned so I couldn't see his face. I gave him some time.

"Doc?"

"Yes Pete?"

"Doc, would you still make a house call? I just can't bear the thought of bringing Groucho down to the clinic. I want to let him go at home."

It occurred to me I had no idea where Pete lived. In his client record was a P. O. Box. "Yes, Pete, I could do that. When?"

Pete turned around, "Tonight?"

"I've a full afternoon schedule, I won't be done till six. It would have to be after that."

"That would be all right. Thanks, Doc. I mean it."

"You better tell me how to get there."

"Right. Uh, sure, Doc."

"Let's go inside so I can write down directions." I found out that Pete didn't live in Willits. He lived just north of Laytonville, a town twenty miles north of Willits. After I wrote down the directions, he gave me his cell phone number.

"Now, Doc, when you get to the first gate, you call

that number, and I'll have Joey come down to unlock the gate."

"Okay, Pete. I'll call you when I get ready to leave Willits and then again when I get to the gate. It probably won't be until seven thirty."

"Whatever time you get there will be fine, Doc."

He put his hand out, and I shook it. He held fast.

"Doc, Thank you. This really means a lot to me."

"I'll see you tonight, Pete."

As I drove north that night, I realized I hadn't told anyone where I was going. As darkness drew in, I started to wonder if I should be worried. *Oh, come on, I told myself you've known Pete for fourteen years.*

I pulled up to the gate that had a large chain and padlock on it. I called Pete's cell phone, and he said Joey was already on his way and soon I saw headlights approaching from the other side. Joey parked his truck, opened the gate and walked over to me.

"Drive on in, Doc, and wait for me."

I drove my truck in while Joey locked the gate behind me. He came up and got in the passenger seat. *Did I really see a gun under his coat? Oh my God, why didn't I tell anyone where I was going?*

"Doc, just drive up this road, but when I tell you to stop you really need to stop."

Suddenly it seemed very warm in the cab, I opened my window. We drove about two miles before Joey told me to stop. I stopped.

"Stay in the truck." I did. Joey got out. He pulled a long flashlight from under his coat; the gun I thought I'd seen. He turned it on and started to wave it around, at the same time he was yelling, "Friend! Friend! Friend!"

He did this three times and got back into my truck. "My mistake, Doc, we should have used my truck. People know my truck."

We went through two more gates and each time Joey repeated his chant.

"Take the right up ahead, Doc. We're almost there." We came to the fork, and I took the one to the right. "We'll be fine now, Doc, this is Pete's and my place." I soon saw a campfire up ahead. "Pull just to the left up there. You'll see Pete's Jeep." I did, we got out of the truck and I grabbed my doctor's case. "Follow me, Doc."

Pete was down by the campfire where Groucho was lying on a sleeping bag. Groucho looked up, but he didn't wag his tail this time, and his eyes looked very tired. He'd lost a lot more weight, and the bones of his face were prominent. Pete stood up.

"I thought I could stay here, Doc, but I just can't." He bent down to Groucho; whispering something to Groucho. Groucho licked his face, and Pete hugged him one last time. As he walked past me, I could hear him sobbing. I looked at Joey, and he nodded.

I patted Groucho as I gave him a sedative. Once the sedative took effect, I put a tourniquet on Groucho's front leg and found his vein, releasing the tourniquet I injected the euthanasia solution. He passed peacefully. Joey had his hand on my shoulder.

"He's gone, Doc?"

I stood up. "Yes, Joey, he is."

"That's good, Doc. It was his time."

"Joey, do you need any help with Groucho?"

"No, Doc, I dug a grave earlier today. It's all ready."

I started walking toward Pete, but Joey grabbed my arm. I turned to him. He just shook his head. "Not a good time, Doc. He needs to be left alone." I nodded.

"Are you ready, Doc? I need to drive back with you."

Again on the drive back, we stopped at each gate, and Joey called out each time. We finally came to the last gate, and Joey let me through. "How much do we owe you, Doc?"

"Nothing, Joey. Pete's been a good client for a long time. Tell him he owes me nothing."

Joey shook his head and proceeded to lock the gate behind me. As I drove back to Willits I was thinking that whether we are teachers, shop owners or "crop" growers, people who love pets share one thing in common—losing a pet breaks your heart. Pete was no different in that regard.

Sometimes after attending a euthanasia, I would get a card of thanks but I heard nothing from Pete. I never saw Pete or Joey again after that night. I later heard that they had been arrested for growing marijuana.

Years later, while I was having lunch, I was going through my mail. There was a small envelope with no return address. I opened it and took out a card and found five crisp $100 bills. It was from Pete:

Dear Dr. Freed,

I hope you remember me. I'm sorry that it has taken me so long to Thank You. At first it was just too painful to even think about Groucho. But now I've had plenty of time to think about a lot of things. Lately,

I've realized that I don't have a lot of friends. Joey told me that night you didn't want any money, but I know you went out of your way to help Groucho and me. You were there for us and I realize now, what that really means. I hope to see you some day, but for now I want to thank you for your kindness and what it meant to me. I think about you a lot. Groucho and I were lucky to have you for our vet.

    Sincerely,
    Pete Larsen

Lunch with the Cats

House call: Towers' cat, Lizzy, behavior change.

I'd received another call from Mrs. Towers. "Dr. Freed we have a new kitty." This brought their household up to eighteen indoor cats. "She is acting funny. Could you see her?"

After I'd agreed to vaccinate their cats at their home last year, I was destined to do house calls there for any ailment. Each time I went, I was astounded at the number of cats and the amount of cat hair everywhere. Recently, Mr. Towers had told me that he'd been covering his computer and camera equipment with sheets of plastic to protect them from "accidents."

"Yes, Mrs. Towers, I'll come by Saturday, late morning. How would eleven be?"

"Why that would be fine, Dr. Freed, and I'll make a nice lunch for you."

The thought of eating in their hair-strewn house, with plastic sheets of dried urine, while eighteen cats climbed everywhere was not appealing. I liked home cooking, but as far as the Towers were concerned there were no boundaries for their cats. Cat hair was everywhere.

"No, No, Mrs. Towers, please don't go to any trouble."

"Why, Dr. Freed, that's the least I can do for you. We appreciate your coming out to our house to care for our kitties."

And so I looked forward to lunch with the Towers on Saturday.

•　•　•　•

I packed my doctor's bag and began my drive to the Towers'. As I drove down Valley Road, I once again saw flocks of turkeys. Today the males were showing their full feathers to attract the females. I stopped to watch. The spring flowers were just coming out with orange poppies and azure lupines. The fields were turning red with the blossoms of new clover.

My drive was interrupted at the train tracks while the Skunk Train passed by pulling passenger cars and open observation cars, on its trip to Fort Bragg.

It would wind through the coastal redwood forest following the Noyo River below. The Skunk Train actually started as the California Western "Skunk" Railroad. It's a picturesque steam engine that takes excursions each weekend, during the summer. The Skunk also runs special events such as the evening Valentine ride where chocolates and champagne are served and the Christmas Run with Santa and carolers.

The journey on the railroad as it twists and turns through the peaceful and inspiring redwoods is a trip to remember. Some of these coastal redwoods are over three hundred feet tall, with diameters up to twelve feet. The railroad started in 1885 building slowly from Fort Bragg and was completed to Willits in 1911. There are forty miles of tracks with grades of up to 3.3%. A feeling of that time has been preserved by the Willits' Roots of Motive Power. This group of railroad enthusiasts has acquired, restored, and exhibit many steam engines and logging equipment once used in the local forests. They are proudly stored in the new facility next to the Willits Museum.

I waved to the tourists as they passed. It made me smile. Here I was living in a place where many people came to vacation. What with the Skunk Train, the Roots of Motive Power, the Willits' Fourth of July Rodeo, and the famous Seabiscuit Ridgewood Ranch there was a lot of history here.

I finally pulled up to the little white cottage. From the outside, with its fresh paint and well cared for garden, no one could realize the chaos inside.

Once again I used the woodpecker shaped doorknocker to announce my arrival. The front door opened about one inch. I could hear Mrs. Towers.

"Are you ready, Dr. Freed?"

I was ready. "Yes."

The door opened some more, I quickly squeezed in, and it shut instantly behind me. There, before me were cats: small cats, longhaired cats, skinny cats, and fat cats. Cats on the floor, on the steps to the second floor, on the tables, chairs, under the sofa, on the sofa, the dining table, the kitchen countertops, wherever the eye would wander there was a cat.

And in the midst sat a smiling Mr. Towers holding a beautiful, purring tabby.

"Is this your newcomer?"

Mr. Towers was obviously proud. "Oh yes, Dr. Freed. I found her when she was only this big." He held his palm out. "She was no bigger than this."

"How long ago, Mr. Towers?"

He looked at his wife, who stepped over and petted the kitten. "That would've been December, so she is about five-months-old. Oh, Dr. Freed, this is Lizzy."

"Well, what seems to be wrong with Lizzy?"

Mr. Towers pulled a page from his desk. Looking it over he said, "Lizzy is quieter now. She sleeps a lot, she use to run all over the place. She has put on a lot of weight. I'm worried she might have cancer."

"Is she eating?

"She can't get enough."

"Is she vomiting?"

"No, nothing like that."

"Well, let's examine her and see what I can find."

We moved some papers and books from a table

and perched Lizzy up on that. While Mrs. Towers held Lizzy, I began my exam. It didn't take long for me to find that Lizzy was pregnant. Now, I knew all seventeen cats were spayed or neutered and I knew the Towers never let their cats out.

"Does Lizzy go outside, Mrs. Towers?"

Both Mr. and Mrs. Towers shook their heads. "Now, you know how we feel about that. Our babies never go outside. We live too close to the road."

"And Lizzy was just a baby when you brought her in?" I asked.

"Fit right in the palm of my hand, with room left over." Mr. Towers smiled at me.

"I can't figure this out because I think Lizzy is pregnant."

"Pregnant!" They both said. "Why, that's impossible!"

"Well, let me examine her again." As I reexamined Lizzy a young tabby, a splitting image of Lizzy, ran by me and up the stairs. As it went up the stairs it was obvious to me it was a young male cat. I looked at the Towers.

"Mrs. Towers, Mr. Towers, you didn't tell me you had a male cat now. No wonder Lizzy is pregnant."

The shook their heads and turned pale.

"Mrs. Towers, I distinctly saw a young male cat just run up those stairs."

She looked at me with a cold, hard stare. "Dr. Freed that cat is Mr. Beautiful, and there is no way he got our Lizzy pregnant. That's her brother!"

And that made nineteen indoor cats with more kittens on their way, and I still had lunch to look forward to.

The Willits Creamery

Thursday 12:30 p.m.: Willits' Creamery.

I was coming out of the Bank of Willits when I looked up to see three women talking. One of them had familiar red curls. Hazel. One of the others, Cyndi Orenstein, had her dog Sadie in my clinic with pancreatitis two weeks before. Sadie was a Miniature Schnauzer and unfortunately these wonderful pets are susceptible to developing pancreatitis secondary to hyperlipidemia: too much cholesterol in their blood. Thanks to Sadie, this gave me a good excuse to walk up to them.

"Hi, Dr. Freed."

"Hi, Cyndi, how is Sadie doing?"

"She's just fine, now that we have her on that special diet. I can't remember the last time she acted so well. She is even playful again."

"Well, I'm glad to hear that. You should bring her in soon to have her pancreatic enzymes rechecked and see if her lipidemia has resolved."

"I'll call your office, Dr. Freed."

"Hi, Charlie." Hazel was standing there with those beautiful eyes cast on me. The sun was shining on her red hair, and her skin was so smooth with just the slightest tan that made small freckles appear around her lips.

"Hi, Hazel. Did you just have lunch?"

"No, Joan and Cyndi were just on their way." Hazel was smiling; perhaps she already knew my intentions.

"Hazel, would you care to join me? I'm just on my way to the Creamery." I had my fingers crossed behind my back.

Hazel looked at Cyndi and Joan. "Would you mind terribly if I didn't join you today?"

Cyndi and Joan were in unison, "Hazel, you go ahead. We'll catch up later on our gossip." They both smiled. "See you later, Dr. Freed."

I smiled. "Thank you." Hazel and I walked across the street and down the sidewalk towards the Creamery. I held the screen door open to the Creamery, and Hazel and I walked in. Immediately, I sensed we were on stage as sidelong glances came our way. I noticed that Mr. Thorten, the president of the Bank of Willits, again occupied the window seat. Down the counter to my left sat Andy Conner, a local California Highway Patrol Officer, and next to him was Lou Stevens, owner of the Willits Shoe Store.

We sat down at the brown-varnished wooden counter; directly across from us stood a Westinghouse refrigerator, which looked like it had been there since the Creamery first opened. Hand-made wooden shelves held glasses for ice-cream sodas and Coca Cola, Root beer, and Orange Nehi. A large six-door freezer for ice cream took up most of the wall and to the left of that was the sink and counter for the three Hamilton Beach mixers for shakes and malts. The sign proudly announced sandwiches of tuna, deviled egg, cheese and ham, all made with white Wonder bread. Price of soda was $0.95, milk shakes $1.15, sundaes $0.85, and banana splits $2.25. At the end of the counter to the left, was a small wood burner stove for the winter days, but today some deep purple irises in a tall green vase were placed on top of it. On the back wall hung a Coca Cola sign with the picture of a pretty blonde, hairstyle 1950's, enjoying her glass of Coca Cola. The whole atmosphere made you feel like you were sitting in a time capsule.

"Dr. Freed, Hazel." Eunice was standing in front of us. "What would you like today?"

"Hi, Eunice, I'd like a ham sandwich and a strawberry shake."

"Hazel?"

"Hi, Eunice, I'll have a chocolate shake and half of

Charlie's sandwich. Oh, maybe a bag of potato chips too."

"Half of my sandwich?"

"Do you mind, Charlie?"

Hazel didn't know it, but I was happy that she felt comfortable with me to do that. No, I didn't mind at all. "Suits me, Hazel."

Soon conversation was going again and our lunch was ready.

"Hazel, I don't think I ever thanked you for inviting me for Christmas dinner."

She was sipping her shake. "Charlie, I'm glad you came. I should've invited you over again. My mom and dad ask about you often."

"Anytime, Hazel."

"Charlie, what're you doing this Friday?"

"You mean after work?"

"Yes. You know I volunteer at St. Anthony's dinning hall, and we're having our annual soup and sip to raise money. We'll be serving all sorts of soups to taste, and we always need help with that."

"You mean you'd like me to help out?"

"Well, you can also taste the soups too."

"Would I be with you all evening?"

She was smiling now. "Yes."

"What time do you want me there?"

"We start serving at six o'clock. Could you be there by five thirty?"

"I'll make it a priority."

I shared my sandwich with Hazel and ate some of her potato chips. While we were there, a young girl and her mother came in.

"Hi, Eunice, Ernestine, Lenora."

"Hello, Mrs. Marshall, and how are you, Judy?" Eunice bent down to little Judy. "Now what do you have there?" Judy handed a piece of paper to Eunice.

"Dr. Thomas said to give this to you." Judy was smiling.

Eunice showed the note to her sisters. "Well, Judy it says here that you had surgery, and you were a very brave girl. Dr. Thomas has prescribed an ice cream cone for you."

Hazel was elbowing me. "Dr. Thomas is the local pediatrician, and he often writes prescriptions for the kids to get an ice cream after their surgery."

Lenora was holding a cone. "Judy what kind of ice cream do you want?"

"I'd like strawberry."

Lenora handed her the ice cream cone. Mrs. Marshall looked at Judy. "And what do you say?"

"Oh, thank you. Thank you for the ice cream cone."

"What kind of surgery did you have, Judy?" Eunice was watching Judy enjoying her ice cream.

Mrs. Marshall spoke up, "Judy had her tonsils removed last week. We're just now getting around to coming in."

"Well, Judy, we're all glad you feel good. Enjoy your cone."

Mrs. Marshall and Judy waved as they left the Creamery.

"You know, Hazel, I like living in a small town."

"Charlie, I'm glad you do." She put her hand on my shoulder as she stood up. "See you Friday."

"I'll be there." I watched her go out the door and walk past the large front window. Lenora came out and sat down next to me. "You know Hazel and Dr. Davison split up."

"Yes."

"Do you know she's been talking about you?"

"To you?"

Oh yes, hasn't she girls?" They were standing around me now. Andy was leaving, and he stopped by on his way out.

"Be careful, Doc. I've seen them do this before. If you don't watch out, they'll have you married in no time."

I sat there finishing my strawberry shake. I thought of Hazel sleeping on my couch that rainy night, how she helped keep me from making a fool of myself at the rodeo, how kind she had been when I fell flat on my face in the mud the first time I saw her, and that wonderful Christmas dinner with her folks. I liked Hazel, and I couldn't wait for Friday night. As for getting married, it was something I was already thinking about.

Willie's Story

Tuesday 3:00 p.m.: Anthony's three puppies, health exams.

I was examining three toy poodle puppies for their first vaccinations. Their little black noses and brown eyes looked like little buttons. The mother, Precious, was attentive, kind, and very friendly. The proud owner stood opposite me.

"Mrs. Anthony, these are three of the cutest puppies I've seen in a long time." Each puppy was vying for my attention, and I petted them and rubbed their bellies as I talked. "Have you named them?"

Mrs. Anthony picked up one of the puppies. She hesitated and smiled at me. "Just for now, this one is Peaches, that one is Princess, and that one is Peter." She smiled. I knew she had named them.

I felt she would've kept them all, but she was on a limited budget and selling these puppies would bring much needed money into her household. I examined the puppies' eyes, ears, and mouths, took their temperatures and listened to their hearts. I'd finished my examinations on Peaches and Princess and then looked up to Mrs. Anthony.

"These two look just great. Let me see Peter." She handed over the little beige bundle to me.

Lisa was helping me with the examinations. When I got to Peter's heart I continued to listen. It wasn't a normal heartbeat; it was what we call a continuous machinery murmur, most likely to be a patent ductus arteriosus (PDA). Before a puppy is born, its blood is given oxygen by the mother, so the puppy's heart has a blood vessel shunt between the vessel from the heart and the vessel to the lungs, basically bypassing the lungs. Once the puppy is born this shunt closes, allowing normal circulation of blood into the lungs to get oxygen. If this shunt doesn't close then most of the blood bypasses the lungs and doesn't get oxygenated. Eventually this can lead to heart failure.

I listened a little longer.

"Is something wrong, Dr. Freed," Mrs. Anthony said in a worried voice.

I took my stethoscope from Peter's chest and looked up at her. "Mrs. Anthony, I'm afraid that Peter has a heart problem. He will need an ultrasound of his heart to determine what kind."

Mrs. Anthony picked Peter up and held him in her arms. "What does an ultrasound cost?"

"It'll cost about $160."

"And then what, Dr. Freed? Will his heart get better? Will he need surgery?"

Now the hard part. How is this nice woman going to afford ultrasound and diagnostics, let alone thoracic surgery to repair a heart problem?

"Well, Mrs. Anthony if it's a PDA, there's a surgery to repair that. Once that is done Peter should do fine." I was trying to bring a little hope to my voice.

"Dr. Freed?"

"Yes?"

"Do you do that surgery?"

Now I had to tell her the whole story. I was hoping to let the doctor that did the ultrasound break the news.

"No, Mrs. Anthony, this is a surgery I don't feel I can do. I would refer you to a veterinary surgeon."

She sat down with Peter in her arms. His little black nose pushed up into her neck, and she held him tight. Tears were forming, and I could see she was going to have trouble talking.

She looked up at me. "But Peter seems fine right now, I don't see how this could be such a problem. He's running and playing with his sisters. They're so much fun to watch." She was trying to smile, hold Peter, and wipe her tears, all at the same time.

"Well Mrs. Anthony, what happens is that while Peter is small his heart can keep up with him, but as Peter grows his heart won't be able to supply enough blood to his lungs to give him oxygen. He will tire easily, maybe cough, eventually he will go into heart failure." She was crying now, and I handed her some Kleenex. I felt awful because I was not a veterinary surgeon—just a run-of-the-mill general practitioner. I knew she wasn't going to be able to afford what needed to be done.

"Why don't you take all your babies home? Here is

the telephone number of the doctor that does the ultra-sound. Why don't we take one step at a time?"

Lisa and I gathered the puppies up and put them in their crate. I watched Mrs. Anthony go out to the front desk and pay her bill. Back in the exam room, I looked out the window as she walked to her car; Lisa carried the puppy crate out for her. Mrs. Anthony got into her car and sat for a while. I watched her pat her eyes again and felt like going for some Kleenex myself. She sat in her car for some time and then finally drove away.

• • • •

Two weeks later I called the veterinarian who does the cardiac ultrasounds.

"Hi, Jerry, did you ever see Mrs. Anthony with her puppy Peter?"

"No, Charlie. I got your message and looked for a record, but she never came in. I know she called about prices, but she never set up an appointment."

"I was afraid of that. What do you think will happen if Peter really has a PDA?"

"Well, it won't take much longer to find out. As he grows, he will start having problems. He will collapse with the slightest exercise. I would expect her to be calling you within the next three weeks."

"Thanks, Jerry. I knew money was a problem, and I didn't expect her to go for it. Have you ever done a PDA surgery?"

"No, I refer any case like that to the specialty clinics; there is one in Rohnert Park and another in Santa Rosa. Sometimes they go to the U. C. Davis Veterinary School."

"Yeah, me too. Well, thanks, Jerry."

That night after work, I sat in my office reading up on the surgical procedure in my veterinary textbooks. I made some notes and reviewed the anatomy of the area. I hadn't done a thoracic surgery since veterinary school, and I didn't feel I was up to it. Although somewhat straightforward, it still involved opening the chest cavity, finding the patent vessel on the beating heart without damaging any associated nerves and having a technician do assisted breathing for the patient. It was better for a surgeon, with a surgical team, to take care of Peter. I closed my books.

After a few weeks of not hearing from Mrs. Anthony and not seeing any of the puppies for their second vaccinations I finally called her.

"Mrs. Anthony? This is Dr. Freed." Silence. "I was calling to see how Peter is doing."

I heard a chair scrape across the floor and in the background puppies playing.

"Hello, Dr. Freed. I just don't know what to do. I was too embarrassed to come back to see you, so I had Dr. Niles do the second puppy shots on Peaches and Princess. They go to their new homes this week."

"And Peter? Do you still have Peter?"

She was sobbing. "Dr. Freed, it's just like you said. As he gets bigger Peter just can't keep up. Right now his sisters are playing, but he just lies there. When he stands he wobbles and falls down. His appetite is good, but he is getting weaker daily and two days ago he started to cough."

"What are you going to do with Peter?"

"Dr. Freed, I just can't afford to do those procedures and surgery. I just can't. I was thinking of having Dr. Niles put him to sleep."

At that moment, I knew what I had to do. "Mrs. Anthony, would you sell Peter to me?"

"What? You want Peter?"

"How much are you selling his sisters for?"

"I am selling them for $350 each, but I wouldn't feel right taking money from you for Peter. If you can help him, I'll just give him to you and you do what you can."

"I can't promise you anything, Mrs. Anthony. Peter could die during surgery. I've never done one of these surgeries before."

"I know, Dr. Freed, but he can't go on like this."

I agreed, and we arranged for Mrs. Anthony to bring Peter in the next morning.

Peter was unable to stand and just lay on the exam table. Mrs. Anthony had already left the clinic in tears. Terry and I looked at each other.

"He isn't going to make it, is he, Doc?"

"Well, Terry we can euthanize him right now or try surgery. But if we're going to try it will have to be tonight."

Terry picked up Peter and hugged him. "I'll call my husband so he'll know where I'll be and this afternoon I can get dinner ready for him and the kids."

We put Peter on a heating set-up in the kennel room. At lunchtime, I reviewed all my notes on the surgery. Lisa was working the afternoon and Terry had explained to her our plans for Peter.

"What time do you want me to come back?" Terry was putting her coat on.

"Our last appointment is at five thirty. Let's plan to start at seven. That way you can get the surgery room ready while Lisa gets a chance to eat something. I'll have Lisa handle the anesthesia and assisted breathing, and I would like you to be my surgical assistant."

"I'll be back at six thirty."

When we finished the day's appointments I went back to my desk with a cup of coffee taking a last look at my textbooks and notes. At seven o'clock we started surgery. The surgery took one and a half hours. It was fascinating working on the vessel while Peter's heart was beating and Lisa was doing assisted breathing for him. We had to coordinate our movements so that the lungs were not obscuring the surgery site as I manipulated the vessel and the instruments.

I looked up at Lisa and Terry. "I have the PDA vessel isolated, and the two ligatures are in place. I'll start to tie the ligatures and Peter's heart should begin beating normally." The heart and oxygen monitors were displaying their respective readings, and the heart monitor had an audible sound so we were all intent on listening as the ligatures were tied securely in place.

Whoosh. Whoosh. Whoosh. And then as the ligatures were tied.

Lub dub. Lub dub. Lub dub.

Our smiles were hidden behind our surgical masks, but I felt a heavy burden exiting the surgery room.

Terry was first, "You did it, Doc! Peter's heart is beating normally!"

We were all silent again; just listening to Peter's little heart.

"Now, Lisa, I am going to start closing up Peter's

chest. Keep breathing for Peter and I'll tell you what I want you to do when I get close to the last suture."

I continued bringing the ribs into position. "Now, Lisa, I want you to give Peter a breath, and I'll tell you how much to expand his lungs." I watched as his lungs were inflated and made sure they looked normal. "Now hold that with his lungs expanded while I tie the last suture. Okay, it's done; let's see if Peter can breathe on his own."

We waited. Nothing. I could see on the monitor that his oxygen level was starting to drop. I was just getting ready to have Lisa begin breathing for Peter, when all of a sudden he took a large breath and exhaled. The monitor beeped. There was a pause and then another beep. Peter could breath on his own, and his heart had a normal beat.

The rest of the skin closure was routine, but the excitement in the room was anything but ordinary. We were ready to jump around and yell, but we didn't. Lisa and Terry continued their monitoring and assisting with the surgery until we were finished. I took off my surgery mask and looked at them both. "Lisa. Terry. I couldn't have done this without you. You both did a terrific job."

Peter woke up from the anesthetic, but I'd given him pain medication so he slept peacefully. I checked on him through the night, and he slept well, breathing normally and his heart rate was stable.

The next morning I noticed Terry's car already in the parking lot as I drove up.

"Terry? You must've gotten up pretty early to beat me to the clinic."

"I couldn't wait to see how Willie was."

"Willie?"

"Doc, he is wagging his tail and begging for food. I haven't fed him yet, waiting for you to check him out, but he's really acting normal."

"Did you say Willie?"

Terry looked at me. "Doc, if any dog has ever had the will to live, it's this little guy right here."

And so we all started to call our little patient Willie.

Willie recovered from surgery and his heart was normal, but he did have some neurological problems that were not obvious before surgery. He'd been too weak for us to see those signs. A referral to a neurologist told us that this was most likely part of a congenital disorder along with the PDA. The neurologist told us that although Willie wouldn't get worse he would always have some neurological symptoms. This doesn't affect his personality, which is sweet and affectionate, but more in his locomotion. Willie was adopted by one of my clients where he continues to delight them with his loving and gentle manner.

A Special Pet

Once you have enjoyed the love of a pet, you will
feel empty without it.

C. A. FREED

For every pet owner there comes along one pet that
becomes the best one they ever had. There is no particular characteristic that makes a pet so special. It's a
composite of traits. It can be a cat or a dog, a horse or a
bird, a rabbit or a rat. There is no way of knowing when
or where this will happen. It just does.

One morning, I drove up to my clinic, and there to
my surprise, a dog sat on the porch. She was a beautiful
Border Collie. As I walked up to the porch she began
to wag her tail like we were old friends and yet I'd never
seen her. When I unlocked the door she walked into
the clinic as if it was her home. At first I put her in
my kennel room, in one of the larger kennels with a
blanket, water, and food. But she would have none of

that. She clawed at the kennel door until I was afraid she would break her nails. I then put her in an outdoor kennel run where she immediately commenced to pull at the kennel wire with her teeth that I was afraid she would break her teeth. She ended up that day in my office, on a blanket where she slept all day.

That afternoon someone called inquiring about a lost dog. Her name was Betty. Sure enough, when that person showed up, this was his dog and home she went.

A few days passed, and all was forgotten until one morning I drove up to my clinic, there was Betty sitting on the porch. This time I knew what to do. She came back to my office, and again I laid a blanket down for her. She ate a dog biscuit, drank some water, and then lay down and went to sleep. This time I had her owner's telephone number and later that day, home she went.

A few weeks went by, and again, one morning as I drove up to the clinic, I saw a friendly wagging tail. Betty was back. After talking with the owner and finding out that his living arrangements had recently changed, it was decided that I could be a foster pet owner for a while. Needless to say she stayed. But not only did Betty stay, she also became my shadow, constantly wanting to be in sight of me. During the workday, she would calmly sleep in my office. But if I went to lunch, she had to go with me. On the weekends she wasn't content to lie around the house, but went everywhere I went. If I mowed the lawn, she couldn't just lie in the shade and watch, she had to walk every step with me, just behind me. Back and forth, back and forth. I would stop, walk her to a shady spot, make her lie down, but as soon as I started to mow again, she was right behind me. At home, I made a place for her to lie down by the dining room table where she would look up at me as though she was grateful for her bed. She loved vegetables and fruit. In the summer we would eat watermelon together. She was unique.

One time Betty rode over with me to Colusa, California, to check on a car for sale and another time went with me to Pittsburg, California, where I picked up a car I had bought. I felt I had a true friend. Pictures of walks on the Fort Bragg beach line my office. And many more pictures are in my scrapbooks at home.

Betty was an older dog when she came to my clinic. I had to treat her for Heartworm disease and for Lyme disease. One day I noticed she was scooting, that usually means a problem with the anal glands, but when I went to clean them I discovered a mass. She went to surgery—the mass was malignant—and I knew in time that she would have problems. It was difficult to play with her and love her, knowing all along that I'd lose her to a disease that was silently going through her body.

First it was a cough. I radiographed her chest and saw the metastatic lesions of the tumor. For a while, medication relieved her cough. Then the fevers started. I got things under control for about three more months, but then one morning, around five thirty, she left her bed in the dinning room and came to my bedroom. She was panting hard and feverish again. She looked up at me for help. I knew what had to be done. I carried this precious dog to my car and drove down to my clinic. I placed her on the exam table and gave her the injection that would allow her peace and stop the struggle to breathe. And then it happened.

As tears where pouring down my face, as I slowly pushed the syringe barrel injecting the euthanasia solution, she looked up at me with those eyes. She picked up her opposite paw and placed it on my hand that held the syringe and then she laid her head down on that paw and passed away.

I hope she was saying thank you for a wonderful few years. I hope she was saying thank you for releasing me from this disease. I hope she knew how important she was to my life and how much I loved her and how much she would always be missed.

As my head came down on top of her and I began to sob, Terry closed the exam room door.

Epilogue

I was sitting in my office. Terry had called and rescheduled the day's appointments. I was staring at a picture of Betty running on the Fort Bragg beach. She was running down by the waves, sea foam on her legs. She looked happy. I heard a faint knock on my door.

"Charlie, Charlie, you okay?"

It was Hazel. I heard the door open.

"Charlie, Terry called me and said what happened." Hazel put her hand on my shoulder; I knew she was looking at the picture of Betty. "I'm sorry."

I replied with a tearful voice, "I couldn't let her suffer."

"You gave her a good life, Charlie. She loved you."

I shook my head. Hazel put her chin on my head. "Charlie, let's go to the coast for the day."

We bundled up and walked out to the parking lot. Flo Anderson was just pulling in; she would've been my first appointment this morning. She came up to me and hugged me. "Dr. Freed, Terry called me, but I just had to come down anyway. You lost Betty?" I nodded. "You take care of yourself, Dr. Freed. I'll see you another day."

"Thank you. It was kind of you..."

She smiled and got back into her car, waving as she drove away.

"Let me drive." Hazel opened her car door.

We drove down Main Street passing under the Willits' arch "Gateway to the Redwoods." Waiting at the signal light to turn west onto Highway 20, Andy Conner, passed and waved to us. The light changed and we turned onto Highway 20.

Hazel had the car heater on and the warmth was comforting. I watched the river running along the side of the road and that with the humming of the car engine and staring up at the coast redwoods passing by I started to relax. I looked over at Hazel. Her red curls where escaping under her wool cap, and I could see the faint freckles on her cheek. She briefly glanced over at me.

"What?"

"This was a good idea, Hazel."

She put her hand on my leg, giving it a quick squeeze, before grabbing the steering wheel again. "I know."

I leaned my head back and felt my eyes blink a few times before falling off to sleep.

Note from the Author

Willits is a small, rural town in Mendocino County of Northern California. It is the home of the Skunk Train, the Forth of July Rodeo, Roots of Motive Power, and Ridgewood Ranch, home of the racehorse legend Seabiscuit.

If you are interested in learning more about:

Willits—Willits' Chamber of Commerce: www.willits.org

The Willits' Creamery—Mendocino County Museum: www.co.mendocino.ca.us/museum

Seabiscuit/Ridgewood Ranch—Seabiscuit Heritage Foundation: www.seabiscuitheritage.org

Willits' Roots of Motive Power: www.rootsofmotivepower.com

Willits' Skunk Train: www.skunktrain.com

Passing in the Night

It is too quiet, there is something wrong, I awake
from a sound sleep
It is so dark I can't see but I reach my hand down to
your place and it is empty
I lie back and listen but nothing comes to my ears
I open and close my eyes and try to think what that
means
My feet make it to the side of the bed and I am
soon up
I call your name but remember you haven't heard me
in such a long time
But still no noise, no loud breathing, no scratching
sounds, no snoring
It is too quiet, there is something wrong and I make
my way down the stairs
I check your spot by my chair but it is empty too
So I wander about the living room, feeling all the
usual places

My hands touch nothing and I head for the
kitchen
I find you next to your food dish, both are cold
I stand still and let that sink so ever slowly into my
sleep weary mind
It is too quiet, there is something wrong and you
are gone
I feel wetness on my face and realize I am crying
making no sound
I sit down next to you and lay my head down on
your still chest
I lay there thinking of all the years that have gone
by
Smiles and tears come one after the other as I
remember your silly ways
Your dancing at dinner time, your chases across the
garden, your bark
It is too quiet, there is something wrong and you
have left me
I hold on to you and cradle you in my arms still sitting on the floor
I look up and your other friend has found us and she
hugs us both
I can feel her sobs, her tears fall on my head and I
hold you even tighter
I lay you down on your bed and cover you with your
blanket
We hug each other over you and tell each other it
is okay

You were old, and tired, and sore, and loved
We slowly climb the stairs back to our bed
It is too quiet, you are gone, but oh so loved.

C. A. FREED